THE POST OFFICE

THE
POST OFFICE

FROM CARRIER PIGEON
TO CONFRAVISION

Nancy Martin

*With 38 photographs and
16 illustrations in text by*
CHARLES GREEN

LONDON
J. M. DENT & SONS LTD

Made in Great Britain
by the
Aldine Press · Letchworth · Herts
for
J. M. DENT & SONS LTD
Aldine House · Bedford Street · London
First published 1969

SBN: 460 06602 1

Contents

Illustrations

For L. B.

who was a telecommunications engineer

Acknowledgments

Most of the information for this book has been obtained through the courtesy and co-operation of Post Office officials who have been interviewed. Visits have been made to the Earth Station at Goonhilly Downs, the Post Office Tower, Dollis Hill Research Station, the *Monarch* cable ship, Fleet House, Norwich and Mount Pleasant Sorting Offices, the Post Office Railway, the National Postal Museum, and various other postal and tele-communications centres.

Publications issued by G.P.O. Headquarters have provided information regarding the history of the Post Office and its many services. Additional historical facts have been obtained from the book by George Walker, entitled *Haste, Post, Haste,* published by George Harrap & Co., and also from various encyclopaedias.

Photographs have been obtained from the Post Office Photographic Library, and are reproduced by courtesy of H.M. Postmaster-General.

The author gratefully acknowledges her indebtedness to all these sources of information.

Foreword

by the Postmaster-General,

the Rt. Hon. John Stonehouse, M.P.

A new age has begun this year for Britain's Post Office with the change from Government department to public corporation. The change will enable the two vast businesses of telecommunications and posts to develop according to their individual needs, and in a way that will meet today's—and tomorrow's—increasingly demanding standards.

The Post Office of the future—the near future—will provide the nation with technologically advanced communications systems both in the rapidly expanding telecommunications network and in the still vital postal service.

It is worth remembering that, taken overall, the Post Office is the biggest, and also one of the most advanced, enterprises in the country, employing more than 400,000 people—one in fifty of the nation's work force.

It operates the largest commercial vehicle fleet in the country—60,000 vehicles which travel 500 million miles a year.

Our telephone network is the largest in Europe and the third largest in the world, with nearly 9,000 million telephone calls being made from nearly 13 million telephones this year.

We are the only postal authority in the world to offer a daily service to every delivery point—and there are 20 million of them in the United Kingdom. We handle 36 million postal items every working day, and every day we collect from 100,000 pillar and posting boxes, from 25,000 post offices and tens of thousands of private firms.

In all this the Post Office continues to follow the high tradition of reliability that has always been its aim. Everyone, from childhood to old age, uses the Post Office's services in one way or another nearly every day of their lives. The Post Office's objective will continue to be to serve every one of its millions of customers as efficiently and cheaply as possible.

Nancy Martin gives a broad account of the work of the Post Office without going deeply into technicalities. Her story of the Post Office will reveal many sides of its services and activities which may not have been known to readers before.

House of Commons   JOHN STONEHOUSE
September, 1969

1

The Changing Pattern

The Post Office is one of the biggest industrial organizations in the world. Over seven hundred million pounds is spent annually on communications alone, and this is expanding every year. During the next four or five years the telecommunications capital expenditure programme will be approximately two thousand million pounds, while two hundred million pounds postal capital expenditure is planned for the same period.

Every day throughout the year we send and receive letters, buy stamps and postal orders, register and express letters, draw pensions: in fact, use the Post Office. By means of the tele-printer and telex system, messages are printed and received simultaneously in places as far apart as this country and Australia. With the introduction and increasing use of satellites for telephony, as well as television, by 1970 it will be possible for people in all countries in the world to talk to each other on the telephone at any time of the day or night.

This is a far cry from the time when messages were written with sharp-pointed sticks on tablets of clay, and passed around to be read by the few who could do so; when a quiverful of arrows was sent as a declaration of war, or drums warned of an approaching enemy; when the first letter carrier was a runner or horseman who took the mail all the way to its destination. In the early part of the last century there was still the risk of highwaymen holding up the mail, or the hazard of storms and snowdrifts causing delays and loss as the coach made its long, arduous journey through wild country.

There are many recorded instances of birds being employed to transmit messages. The Romans made use of pigeons in connection with the Olympic Games. By the middle of the twelfth century a regular system of pigeon communication was in operation between some countries. During the Siege of Paris, in 1870, the pigeon post was prominent. Microscopic photography was used to transfer the printed message to film no bigger than one and a quarter inches, yet each film contained two thousand messages of twenty words each. One of these birds arrived in Paris with eighteen films containing four thousand messages. The films were enclosed in a tiny quill and attached by thin wire to the upper part of one of the tail feathers, or to the leg. The films weighed less than one gramme.

In England at this time pigeons were used by newspaper reporters and stockbrokers, with the result that large fortunes were made on the Stock Exchange. As many as six hundred pigeons were used in 1836, by London stockbrokers and custom-house authorities. The birds were so swift that, in summer time, they would fly the one hundred and thirty-five miles from Boulogne to London and arrive by midday, while the Paris mail was not expected until midnight. Only one hundred and sixty years ago, carrier pigeons provided the fastest means of communication. They were, in fact, the swiftest of all messengers until electricity outran them.

But the use of pigeons is insignificant when compared with the vast network of today's communications system, and the speed with which messages and speech can be transmitted through space.

Remarkable feats of vision and research have made possible the three-hundred-year story of the Post Office. Now it is no longer a Government department, but a nationalized corporation; a go-ahead public service industry, with power to make its own decisions, though answerable to Parliament through the Minister of Posts and Telecommunications for its overall stewardship. It is required to make an annual report for presentation to Parliament. The National Corporation, with its own chairman appointed by the Minister, and with a minimum of six members on the Board, has responsibility for the provision of postal and telecommunications services, Giro and remittance services, as well as data processing, broadcasting and television. A Post Office Users' National Council has been set up to consider representations made by the public, and also any major proposals which are related to the main services, and which affect users.

No longer are the staff of the Post Office civil servants. They are Corporation employees. They total nearly half a million.

On the postal side the primary business now, as always, is the handling of letters. Correspondence and parcels pass through the Post Office at the rate of eleven to twelve thousand million items a year, which is approximately seventy times as much as when Rowland Hill inaugurated the penny post a hundred and thirty years ago.

What happens to this huge volume of mail from the time it is dropped into one of the hundred thousand pillar-boxes until it is delivered to the eighteen million homes and offices in this country? What happens to overseas mail? How are telephone calls connected, nationally and internationally? How are submarine cables laid, and what is the purpose of earth stations such as Goonhilly? What is meant by Giro and Confravision?

These are some of the things with which this book endeavours to deal in a non-technical manner.

2

A Retail Shop

The function of the Post Office has developed greatly over the years of its existence. Starting as a place for the receipt and despatch of letters, it is now one of the largest retail businesses in the country; the shop for such Government offices as the Treasury and the Department for Health and Social Security, as well as for local government offices. It serves the public by offering facilities for business transactions of many different kinds, as well as issuing a multitudinous variety of forms, licences, orders and benefits accruing from the social services.

Whereas the first post offices consisted of a few inns set at strategic points in different parts of the country, the increasing variety and number of transactions performed by today's post offices has necessitated the establishment of nearly eighteen hundred Crown offices and over twenty-three thousand sub-offices, known officially as Scale Payment Sub-offices. In the early days of post office history the State employed a postmaster-general with a few postboys, or runners, and a small number of innkeepers as sub-postmasters. Today the total staff employed in the whole of the postal section amounts to one hundred and eighty-nine thousand. With the telecommunications side of the business employing another two hundred and eighteen thousand, it is obvious that the work of the British Post Office is one of major importance.

How is this enormous business organized, and exactly what services does it perform for the public who spend more than seven hundred million pounds a year on the communications services alone?

Most villages in the country have their own sub-post office. When one village office closed recently, a mobile office was started in the back of an official van. For two and a half hours twice a week a full counter service is provided, including the payment of pensions.

The village post office may be no more than a counter in one corner of a general shop, but it performs most of the functions of the Crown office. Any staff which the postmaster (or post-mistress) employs are his responsibility and are not employees of the Post Office.

Postmistresses are often conveniently, and sometimes un-justly, used by writers of fiction as the purveyors of gossip, making themselves acquainted with the contents of postcards and telegrams. Those who write period stories have some justification for this. In the latter part of the sixteenth century it was not uncommon for the postmaster, out of curiosity, to delay the despatch of mail until he had leisure to open and read the letters. With the possibility of threats of invasion, the more scrupulous postmaster sometimes held certain private letters which had come by ship, while he wrote to the Master of the Posts for authority to open them. Today's Post Office employees observe a strict code of ethics about the business passing through their hands. This is one of the conditions laid down in their terms of employment.

The main Crown office is known as the Head Office, and the head postmaster there is responsible for the whole area.

In the head postmaster's area there will be a number of Crown offices, some with sorting facilities, others simply engaged in counter transactions, as well as a large number of scale payment sub-offices.

Everyone is familiar with the customer's side of the counter. Parents draw their family allowances, the elderly their pensions, employers and others purchase national insurance stamps, while nearly everyone buys postage stamps.

Every working day of the year two million people buy postal orders. Add to this the million registered items despatched each week, and two hundred and seventy thousand money orders purchased weekly, and it will be seen how dependent we are on the Post Office for the despatch of money and valuable articles. Against this volume of business it is difficult to imagine the time when it was customary for Treasury notes to be cut in half and sent in two separate envelopes.

Postal orders vary in value from one shilling to five pounds. If they are crossed they can be paid only through a bank. Although this is a safe and much-used means of sending money through the post, an even greater degree of security is effected by the use of money orders. For these, a purchaser must give the sender's name and address, and the name of the payee, and an advice is sent forward to the payee. When the payee presents the order it is matched with the advice and will not be paid unless the sender's name is correctly stated. Money orders can be crossed for payment into a bank, but otherwise the name of the post office through which they are to be cashed must be shown on the form. One of the advantages of the use of money orders is that they can be telegraphed. Sums up to the value of fifty pounds can be sent by a single money order.

Registered mail, which may not be sent by second class post, is becoming less and less used as customers realize that recorded delivery is a much cheaper method of sending important documents through the post. This gives proof of delivery, though it lacks the advantage of the insurance which covers registered packets. For this service an additional fee of ninepence is charged for both first and second class service, as against the minimum additional sum of three shillings for registration. By payment of an additional ninepence the sender can receive advice of delivery. Anything worth more than two pounds should not be sent recorded delivery, because the Post Office will not pay compensation should it go astray.

Following the Christmas period of 1967 over three hundred claims for loss of money sent by this means had to be refused for this reason.

Both registered and recorded delivery mail must be handed over the counter for despatch and a receipt obtained. There are a number of conditions governing the payment of compensation in the case of loss or damage. A list of these is contained in the *Post Office Guide*, which can be consulted at any post office, or purchased from the same source.

While many items can be sent registered in an ordinary envelope, money must be sent in the registered envelopes which can be purchased at the Post Office, if a claim is to be made in the event of damage or loss. This regulation includes paper money, in which is included stamps, bonds and money vouchers. An additional regulation in the case of paper money requires the furnishing of particulars sufficient for identification before compensation can be given. Parcels or registered packets sent cash on delivery are subject to a trade charge, according to their value, which must not be over fifty pounds. These may not be sent by second class mail.

Now that the Post office has become a National Corporation, savings are no longer its responsibility. Savings accounts of all kinds come under the jurisdiction of the chancellor of the exchequer. This change will not materially affect the public as the Post Office will act as agent for the Treasury by handling the business through individual post offices in the same manner as, for instance, pensions are paid on behalf of the Department for Health and Social Security.

The Post Office Savings Bank came into being just over a century ago as a result of the Industrial Revolution. Workers were encouraged to save while earning and George Chetwynd, a book-keeper in the Money Order Department of the Post Office, who was the originator of the postal order, was the man responsible for evolving the method of administering the Post Office Savings Bank. He it was who invented the deposit book, by means of which money could be paid in and withdrawn

from depositors' accounts on demand. William Ewart Glad-
stone, then chancellor of the exchequer, later to become prime
minister, promoted the Post Office Savings Bank Bill 'to make
good the shortcomings of the Trustee Banks' which had been in
existence for over half a century. He felt that the Post Office
was in a position to make its own Savings Bank safe, cheap and
convenient. He successfully combated opposition from existing
banks, and the Post Office Savings Bank was opened for
business on 16th September 1861.

The venture was well established from the start. Apart from
a few setbacks, such as those caused by the outbreak of war,
progress was maintained, the number of accounts increasing to
more than twenty-two million, with deposits valued at more
than one thousand six hundred million pounds. The advantage
of the Post Office Savings Bank over others at that time, was the
fact that it was the only one which could offer countrywide
coverage with complete security, and withdrawals on demand,
while paying interest at $2\frac{1}{2}$ per cent.

Henry Fawcett, the blind Postmaster-General, who started
the parcel post, was responsible for much of the development of
savings through the Post Office and for the increased number of
post offices handling saving bank business.

National Savings Certificates and Premium Bonds were
another part of the responsibility of the Post Office prior to its
becoming a National Corporation. These also can still be purchased through individual post offices.

National Giro, which came into operation on 18th October
1968, is a new department within the Post Office. It is a
banking service providing business firms, public utilities, local
authorities and other organizations, as well as individuals over
the age of sixteen, with a simple, cheap and quick means of
transferring money. The minimum initial deposit required to
open an account is one pound.

Giro provides facilities for obtaining foreign currency and
travellers' cheques. This can be done by mail through the Giro
Centre at Bootle, Lancashire, free postage being allowed in

both directions. There are also facilities for depositing and withdrawing cash at nearly twenty-three thousand post offices. The Centre had been planned to handle over one million accounts but there is sufficient space on the site to extend the Centre to handle many more than this. Five million pounds was spent on building the Centre and six and a half million pounds on its equipment. The eleven computers and data processing equipment include some of the most modern machinery in the world. The Centre houses one of the largest computer complexes in Europe.

The whole system is geared to the settlement of accounts in the quickest and easiest manner for the account holder. For instance, those who have these accounts can have payments automatically collected and debited when they become due. Thus, when a customer receives an account it will be paid automatically on time without any action being necessary on his part. A statement of account is issued when there is a new credit on his account, when there are ten debits, or when three months have elapsed. For this service there is no charge.

Giro differs from the arrangements which can be made through banks by the fact that the required sums are paid over immediately without the delay of clearing houses. It is similar to payment by the banks' Direct Debit facility, whereby accounts for varying amounts are paid on due date without the necessity for them to pass through the customers' hands, a service which is designed to simplify the work of any company or institution which has to collect varying amounts at different intervals of time from a large number of customers. There is also a free standing order service which will enable Giro account holders to transfer money direct to their own bank accounts.

To pay an account with another Giro member, an account holder simply completes a transfer form showing the amount and the Giro number of the creditor. A Giro directory is provided for this purpose. He then posts the form to the Giro Centre in the pre-addressed envelope provided. No postage is payable and no cheque required. In fact, the transfer will cost the Giro account holder nothing.

A statement will be sent out when the transfer has been made. Those without a Giro account who wish to make payments to account holders can do so through the post office for a charge of ninepence for amounts up to fifty pounds, and two shillings each for amounts in excess of fifty pounds.

A team of consultants is available to potential Giro customers to give assistance with plans to integrate their own accounting systems with the Giro system, with resultant internal economies for the customer.

It is obvious that there are disadvantages as well as advantages in using Giro rather than the usual banking facilities, such as the fact that some services cost more when purchased through Giro. Travellers' cheques for large denominations are one example. As with current accounts at ordinary banks, no interest is paid, but unlike banks, no overdrafts are permitted. The Giro account holder can draw no more than twenty pounds at a nominated post office on any one day, and he may do this only once every other day. Banks impose no limits, but against this must be set the facts that post offices have longer opening hours, and there are nearly twenty-three thousand post offices in all parts of the country handling these accounts, against approximately twelve thousand banks.

When everything is considered, Giro does offer something new in banking. There are sure to be teething troubles, but if it follows the pattern of the Post Office Savings Bank and other services inaugurated by the Post Office, it will perform a very useful function.

Radio and Television Broadcast Receiving licences are issued by the Post Office, but there are a great many people who evade purchasing them, with a resultant loss of about six million pounds a year to the Post Office. It is required of radio and television dealers that they give the Post Office the names and addresses of all who purchase or rent television sets from them. If people have the wrong type of licence the Post Office takes this up with the user by letter, and visits if necessary, to see that the right type is taken out. In addition, Post Office detector vans can be used to pinpoint working unlicensed television sets. The number of these vans has recently been increased, the newest being fitted with the most up-to-date detecting equipment developed by the Post Office. This equipment can locate sets tuned in to any channel, even pinpointing the room in which the set is standing. It is hoped, in this way, to discover and deal with licence dodgers.

A service which the Post Office gives to licence holders is the investigation of complaints of interference on radio and television sets. The service is provided free of charge. A form for the purpose of making such complaints is available at local post offices. Nearly seventy thousand cases of interference are investigated by the Post Office each year, but as suppressors must now be fitted to most items of electrical equipment, this is much less than formerly—in 1955 there were one hundred and seventy thousand. A special team is employed in each area to track these down.

Until the Post Office became a National Corporation, the issue of dog licences was its responsibility. This has now been delegated to local authorities, but the Post Office will sell these if the local authority desires. Driving licences cannot be obtained through the Post Office, though it does issue application forms for these. Car licences can be obtained at some two thousand post offices.

Licences required for operating a postal franking machine, or business reply service, are issued by the Post Office, and numerous stamps and documents, such as those for payment of Death Duty and Land Registry, can be obtained at some post offices.

These, and many other services performed by the Post Office, are everyday events: a part of living which is taken for granted. All this involves a great deal which is unfamiliar to the customer —the work done on the other side of the counter which makes the smooth running of these services apparently effortless and natural.

More and more Crown offices are becoming bright and spacious, with attractive modern fitments and staff ready to give the full range of service at all counter positions. This avoids customers having to queue at more than one position as they did in the past, when stamps, pensions, savings and other services were dealt with at separate counters.

In general, most post offices are open from nine o'clock until five-thirty from Monday to Friday, and from nine o'clock until four-thirty on Saturdays, except on public holidays. A few of the largest offices have longer opening hours. Some of the smaller Crown offices, and many of the scale-payment offices, also close during lunch time in line with shops in the locality. Most scale-payment offices are also closed for one half day a week, while the big office at Trafalgar Square and another at London Airport are always open, even on Christmas Day.

It is obvious that much accounting and stock-taking must be done by counter clerks after business is closed to the public. The week's takings and outgoings must be balanced against stocks of stamps, postal orders and all the other monetary matters dealt with.

Yet this tremendous counter business is but a small part of the function of the Post Office—that of collecting, sorting and delivering the thirty-five million letters, cards, newspapers and parcels despatched each day. But first let us consider the postage stamp, with its fantastic daily turnover and its world-wide field of operation.

CHAPTER

3

Postage Stamps and Postmarks

The number of philatelists in Britain has more than doubled in the last five years until now it is estimated that one out of every twelve people collects stamps.

As in many things connected with communications, Britain led the way in introducing the first gummed postage stamp. Known as the penny black, it bears a picture of Queen Victoria. It was the first postage stamp in the world and is still the most famous.

Until Rowland Hill put forward his plan for the penny post, the recipient and not the sender paid for letters despatched through the post office. At that time there were areas in England where postmen were never seen and even large towns were without a post office. In fact, the post was so expensive that it was used only when there was no other way of sending a message.

When only ten years of age Rowland Hill was aware of the problem arising from this method. 'I early saw the inconvenience of being poor . . . [my mother] was afraid the postman might bring a letter while she had no money to pay the postage,' he wrote. If an Irish labourer working in England sent a letter home, the cost, including the return postage, was equal to one-fifth of his week's wages. Letters were charged according to mileage, the rates ranging from twopence for distances up to eight miles, to one shilling for three hundred miles. These were the rates for single letters, the charge being doubled if a second sheet were included and tripled for a third. Frequently, in order to avoid the high charges demanded, letters were refused by the recipient and all kinds of subterfuges were practised to obtain news without paying postage. Sometimes the envelope contained a coded message which the recipient read before refusing to accept the letter.

Rowland Hill's famous story illustrates this point. A cottager refused to accept a letter because she could not afford to pay for it, so a sympathetic observer paid the fee for her. When the postboy departed, the woman told her benefactor that he might have saved his money as there was nothing in the envelope. The mere fact that it was sent was sufficient to inform her that her son was well.

In putting forward his advocacy of a small adhesive stamp for prepayment of postage at a uniform rate, regardless of distance, Rowland Hill contended that charges by distance could not be supported economically. He argued that the cost per letter varied not according to distance travelled, but by the number carried, and that a reduction in postage would result in more use being made of the service, with a consequent increase in revenue. His plan for the penny post met with fierce opposition, but eventually parliamentary sanction was given and the penny black came into use in 1840.

The result was an immediate increase in the number of letters despatched, but it was some years before the same could be said of the revenue obtained. Seven years later Rowland Hill was made Secretary to the Post Office and the penny post became really successful. By the time he retired, the volume of mail carried was fifty times as great as before he introduced the penny black, while the receipts for postage had become an economical proposition.

He was, himself, an accomplished amateur artist, and when he wanted his first stamps designed he knew the best men to do this.

The Chief Engraver at the Royal Mint, William Wyon, was one of the outstanding artists of the period. His portrait medallion of Queen Victoria's head was used as the basis for all the adhesive stamps printed during the Queen's long reign. Henry Corbould was selected as the artist and Charles Heath engraved the die from Corbould's line drawing of the Queen's head, taken from the Wyon medal.

It seems strange that the printing of the first postage stamp was done by an American printer, Jacob Perkins. Currency restrictions at that time made necessary the production of vast quantities of bank notes, and it was this which brought Perkins to London. He introduced into the country a turning lathe to engrave the background to the stamps. Intricate white patterns were engraved on steel printing plates and these were extremely difficult to imitate. Perkins revived an ancient process, improving it to suit the mass production security printing necessary for the postage stamp, as well as the bank note. By means of a transfer roller process Perkins produced printing plates, each with two hundred and forty stamp impressions. Thus artist, engraver and printer made an ideal combination for the production of the first British postage stamp.

From the beginning these were produced in sheets of two hundred and forty stamps, twelve in a row and twenty rows deep for ease in accountancy; a method which has survived, though it was not until 1854 that the first official perforated sheets were made. Previously stamps had to be cut from sheets as they were issued and used. The sum of four thousand pounds was paid by the Government for the patent. Marginal perforations vary in number in different countries and stamp collectors often use a special gauge to measure them. Sometimes perforations had to be changed because the stamps separated too easily. Even the gum on the stamp is subject to change. Recently it was found that gum arabic, which comes from acacia trees in Africa, had become too costly. Experiments were made and an alcohol based glue was used. Tests revealed that stamps had better 'lie-flat' qualities with this gum and that it was non-toxic, tasteless and colourless. Its use also resulted in a saving of up to six thousand pounds a year.

Perforated initials are put on stamps by some business concerns as a safeguard against theft.

An attempt to produce a prepaid postal wrapper, or envelope, was at first quite unsuccessful. The illustrated Mulready envelope, named after its designer, was ridiculed everywhere and very quickly taken out of production and replaced by the Penny Pink embossed envelope, the forerunner of the stamped envelopes on sale over post office counters today.

It is interesting to note that, when stamps for different denominations were introduced, colours were selected which would easily be recognized by artificial light as well as by daylight.

Although it became customary for people to buy stamps to prepay postage, Rowland Hill never succeeded in making this a compulsory measure. Even today unstamped letters can be sent, but the recipient will be charged double the normal postage.

Other countries were quick to see the benefits of the postage stamp, and the pioneer work of the two companies who printed the first British postage stamps resulted in a big export trade. This now earns overseas currency to the value of well over one million pounds per annum for the printing of eighteen thousand million stamps.

The mind is baffled by the astronomical figures which cover many of the dealings of the Post Office. Not least of these is the number of stamps sold in this country every year: eight thousand million of them. If these were put end to end they would go round the world about six times.

By far the greater number are sold in sheets. If a large quantity is required they can be purchased in rolls. Many small users take advantage of the convenient books of stamps, ranging in value from two shillings to ten shillings, some of varying denominations. Altogether, with those sold through stamp machines, which are situated outside many post offices, thirty-five million books are purchased annually. This effects a great saving in counter work at the post offices. From decimalization day these machines will continue to accept both shillings and five new pence coins but will issue decimal value stamps.

In rural districts, stamps can be purchased from the postman when he is on his rounds.

Unused stamps, amounting to a pound or more in value, will be repurchased by the Post Office under certain conditions. This applies to stamps which have been spoiled inadvertently, as well as to those in perfect condition. It also applies to stamped stationery. A commission of 12½ per cent is charged for this service.

Various schemes have been devised to assist those who despatch large numbers of postal packets. One is the opportunity to order stamps in advance. If that is done, the Post Office will have them ready for collection the next day.

A deposit account can be opened whereby sufficient money is deposited to cover anticipated postage for a certain period, the depositor agreeing to pay whatever postage may be due at the end of the specified time. Mail is then handed over unstamped.

Where packets of more than one hundred and twenty identical letters have to be posted, they may be paid for in cash, leaving the post office to frank the letters.

The more general practice of large users of the post is to hire or purchase a franking machine and frank the packets on their own premises to whatever value is appropriate. This method is simple and time saving and accounting is automatic. All franking machines sold since June 1968 print the postage values in pence instead of in shillings and pence, as formerly. This is done in readiness for the introduction of decimal currency which takes place in February 1971.

Obviously there are certain conditions regarding the use of these franking machines. They can be obtained only under licence from the local head post office; payment of postage in advance is required; the letters must be faced and tied in packets; the machine meter must be set periodically, and dockets showing daily meter readings submitted weekly.

One big advantage to users of franking machines is that an advertising message can be printed on the envelopes as they are franked for posting.

The business reply card and envelope is another service which the Post Office offers to its customers. This is a useful method of prepaying return postage. A number of conditions apply to the use of these. The envelope or card must comply with certain specified regulations and be submitted to the Post Office for approval before application is made for a licence. A fee of one penny, additional to the normal postage, is charged on each returned card or envelope. For this service the licensee must pay a deposit of such sum as is likely to accrue in one month. When this sum is almost exhausted a further payment is necessary to renew the credit. The amount deposited must not be less than ten shillings.

Letters were postmarked long before the postage stamp was conceived. One of the reasons for postmarking was to 'prevent any neglect of the Letter-carriers in the speedy delivery of Letters'. They were stamped with the town mark, the date of arrival there and the charge. At the end of the eighteenth century mileage from the General Post Office in London was also shown as part of the town mark.

Postal authorities soon saw the advantages of advertising by means of postmarks. One of the earliest examples is that which states—'Essex post goes and comes every day'.

Every year thousands of different new stamps are issued. These include stamps to commemorate important events, such as notable anniversaries and England's victory in the World Cup Football Competition in 1966. In that year also the first two Christmas stamps designed by children were issued. These will surely be added to collectors' treasures. Among the more recent stamps issued are those showing the history and activities of the General Post Office, and the Investiture of the Prince of Wales.

A guiding committee, representative of professional and trade bodies, and including a housewife, meets regularly to consider issues and designs of new stamps. Colour trials are made, as colours are important in making the various denominations easily distinguishable.

A Philatelic Bureau is operated at the General Post Office in Edinburgh. This is of considerable use to collectors because not only does it sell stamps, but also it publishes a monthly bulletin giving details of new stamp issues, as well as other information about postage stamps. There is also a Philatelic Sales Counter at London Chief Office. These together have a turnover of nearly a million pounds a year.

In 1966 a National Postal Museum was inaugurated by the Post Office at London Chief Office, in King Edward Building, King Edward Street, London, E.C.1. This was made possible by the presentation of a valuable collection of British postage stamps owned by Mr Reginald M. Phillips, of Brighton. The donor also gave fifty thousand pounds to maintain the Museum. This collection of nineteenth-century British stamps is considered to be the most comprehensive in the world and is valued at well over a quarter of a million pounds. A great deal of other material has been added, including the registration sheets for almost every postage stamp issued since the penny post was inaugurated.

Accommodation was, at first, very restricted, but a greatly extended permanent museum was opened by the Queen in February 1969. During the first sixteen years of the Queen's reign no less than one hundred and sixty-seven different designs have been issued in this country, as compared with one hundred and twenty-four during the previous one hundred and twelve years. An award, known as the 'Reginald Phillips of Brighton Award for Postage Stamp Design' is to be presented every five years to the artist who has made the greatest contribution to British postage stamp design, the first award being made in June 1969.

The Museum attracts thousands of visitors each year,

including school parties and philatelic groups, for whom lecture tours are arranged.

When Rowland Hill first introduced the postage stamp, he could have had little idea how valuable some of these stamps were to become to the millions of ardent philatelists all over the world. Stamp collecting is a hobby shared by all kinds of people, from the wealthy to the smallest schoolboy, many of whom have quite valuable collections. Numerous stories are told about the way stamps have changed hands, making a small fortune for the owners. Some of these are true only in part.

One such story, which is at least partially true, concerns a schoolboy who owned a one-cent British Guiana stamp dated 1856. Because the boy did not fancy the colour—black on magenta—he gave it to another boy, taking in its place a French stamp of practically no value. Eventually the second boy decided to sell the British Guiana stamp. A sailor friend took it to America on his behalf, where it was known a certain Mr Riley had a similar stamp—the only other of its kind. The American compared it with his own and decided the boy's stamp was a better specimen. He offered the sum of seven thousand pounds, which was gladly accepted. The story goes on to relate that Mr Riley then offered the sailor a cigar, lit one for himself, then burned his original stamp, saying that the stamp which he had just purchased for seven thousand pounds was the only stamp of its kind in the world, and therefore now worth fourteen thousand pounds. But the story does not finish there. When Mr Riley died, his widow disposed of most of his stamps. Those which remained included the British Guiana stamp, which she kept as a memento, much to the frustration of stamp collectors, who would have been willing to pay a very high price for it. Later, Mrs Riley was informed that the stamp was not genuine and therefore worthless. She had it valued by a lawyer, who employed experts to decide the matter. It proved to be a genuine British Guiana stamp of 1856. She decided to sell, and it was purchased for twelve thousand pounds by an unknown man who refused to give his name. The stamp was shown in an exhibition shortly afterwards, but now nobody knows where it is or who is the owner of this unique stamp. The schoolboy who swopped the stamp has now died, but how he must have regretted his unfortunate swop!

Whether or not the story is wholly true, the essential facts are accurate, and this is only one of many similar stories about stamps. Early, unusual, defaced, misprinted or limited issues of stamps have made fantastic prices when sold at stamp auctions.

4

Transporting the Mail

Collections of letters from roadside pillar-boxes started soon after the Penny Post came into being. Today, the little red post van is a familiar sight, though bicycles are still used in some places and, in congested areas, deliveries are often made on foot.

The earliest letter carriers took the letters all the way from the sender to the receiver; they regarded the task as one of the highest importance and often made strenuous efforts to reach their destination. A Greek historian, recording the feats of Persian letter carriers, states that 'neither snow, nor rain, nor heat, nor night stays these couriers from the swift completion of their appointed rounds'. Later, a Greek general remarked that the king's letters travelled more swiftly than cranes in flight. When the Greeks developed their own system of running messengers there were many stories of devotion to duty. These men were famous runners in Olympic games and one of them is said to have run one hundred and fifty miles in a day and a night. Another dropped dead from exhaustion immediately he had delivered his message.

It was not until the sixteenth century that the beginnings of a permanent postal service were really established in this country, with Brian Tuke as the first Master of the Posts, and at that time only the king's mail was carried. Postboys on horseback took the mail in a leather bag strapped behind the saddle. With

(*Above*) Staff handle more than a million parcels a week at Mount Pleasant

(*Top left*) A pneumatic tube system was tried out in 1863

(*Left*) A loaded train in a tunnel of the Post Office Railway

Inside a sorting coach on the Great Western Down

A Travelling Post Office train picking up pouches at speed

Bulky mail goes through the drum to the lower end of the Segregator

Operators feeding and clearing mail from the Automatic Letter facing and stamp cancelling machine

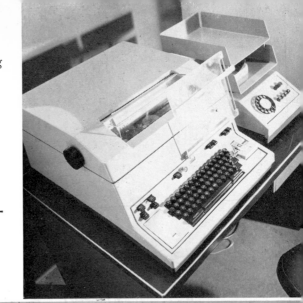

(*right*) Automatic Telex installation with reperforating & tape transmitting attachments

(*Below*) The cordless switch-board on which manually handled international telex calls are dealt

Telephonists at work on a switchboard and, *below*, the
Switchroom of Central Office Westminster Telephone
Exchange, from *The Graphic*, 1883

Many pairs of wires can be carried in one cable. Here a jointer is working on a thousand-pair cable

roads divided into stages of ten to fifteen miles, these postboys were instructed to blow their horn every four miles, or whenever they met other travellers on the road who had to make way for the Royal Mail.

Communication with the rest of the country was almost non-existent, and the arrival of the postboy was quite an event. At the sound of the horn, villagers came from their cottages and crowded around the inn, or post-house, with its swinging post-horn, to listen eagerly to whatever news the postboy could give, and he made the most of his opportunities of telling a good story. The pay for this service was poor, but there were means of making a few extras. Sometimes the boys accompanied royal messengers who gave them a tip as well as a penny a mile for the horse. Today, 'danger money' would be paid for the hazardous duties which fell to their lot, but those ill-clad postboys travelled for miles on the poorest of horses, over lonely marshes or through thickly wooded areas, where gangs of robbers lurked. The roads were only cart tracks, full of potholes, muddy in winter and thick with dust in summer—all practically devoid of signposts. Once the beacon lights were out of view the risk of losing the way was a major hazard.

Towards the end of the sixteenth century, the postboy began to carry private letters, though this was not done officially. When Thomas Witherings became postmaster in 1635, the carrying of private letters became a major function of the newly created State Postal Service. The story of the postal service was one of progress and decline for many years, with roads deteriorating, robbery by highwaymen, and no adequate pay for postmasters or letter carriers. By the middle of the seventeenth century the post office staff had dwindled to forty-five, and of these, thirty died in the Great Plague.

In the later part of the seventeenth century, stage coaches were being used, but it was some time before the postal authorities saw the advantages of using a mail coach and, in spite of the increasing use of the post, London still had no internal postal service. Business houses and private people in London had no means of communicating with each other except by using their own private servants, or by hiring messengers at considerable expense, to act as letter carriers.

It was a London merchant, William Dockwra, who was responsible for changing this state of affairs by establishing a penny post in London in 1680. He set up between four and five hundred receiving points, with fifty letter carriers who called at these points up to twelve times a day. This proved so successful that after about two years the service was taken over by the State and became part of the organized postal system. Later, a number of post collectors were appointed who were really walking letter boxes. They carried a bag with a slot in the side and rang a bell as they walked the streets. Anyone could post a letter in the bag and give the man a penny, which he kept. This was in addition to the normal charge, which was collected from the receiver of the letter.

Even when the mail coach was introduced, in the late eighteenth century, many of the postboys still made journeys on horseback on the lesser roads, which were beset by highwaymen, while the mail coach itself was not immune from these risks. The mail was put in the boot, which was then locked, and the armed guard sat with his feet on it. No one was allowed to sit near him. The guard's seat at the rear of the coach was precarious and, with bad roads and coaches badly sprung, accidents were frequent. One of the journals of the day records such an accident to men working the York coach:

'The coachman and guard were both chucked from their seats going down to Huntingdon last journey, and coming up, the guard is lost from the same cause; the passengers say that he was blowing his horn just before they missed him. A sharp turn, an unexpected obstacle, a too rapid descent, and the absence of the guard may not be discovered until the end of the stage.'

Then there were ice, snow and fog to contend with. Sometimes the coach had to be abandoned when it had gone only half way. The Exeter coach had to be dug out of snowdrifts five times on one journey. The loyalty of many of the mail guards and coachmen was phenomenal. Two such, caught in a snowstorm in Scotland, decided to abandon the vehicle when the horses could not move it any farther. The horses were unharnessed and guard and coachman, accompanied by the postboy, rode on with the mail. Soon the horses became too exhausted to continue the journey, and they were sent back to the posthouse with the postboy. Coachman and guard travelled across the moor on foot, carrying the mail and hoping to reach the next posthouse. A few days later their mail bag was found tied to a tree while, a short distance away, the men lay dead, buried in a snowdrift.

Mail coaches were used for only sixty years, but during the latter part of their existence, roads improved and so did the coaches. By the beginning of the nineteenth century there were twenty thousand miles of first-class roads maintained by the turnpike charges collected at eight thousand gates.

The mail coaches were an impressive sight as they lined up each evening at eight o'clock along the whole of London's Lombard Street, then the headquarters of the postal service. There they waited for the mail bags to be loaded into the boot before they commenced their overnight journeys. Their horses were well fed and groomed, making a very different picture from those used by the postboys. The coaches themselves were inspected each morning and every smallest detail had to be clean and shiny. From the linchpins to the lamps and the coach body itself, the whole thing had to be in perfect order.

The guards, too, presented a very different spectacle from some of the poorly clad postboys of the past. With their scarlet cloth coats, their blue lapels and linings, blue waistcoats and gold-banded hats, the mail coach guards were the most imposing men on the road. Though they were paid only ten shillings and sixpence a week, they made it up to around five hundred pounds a year with tips and special fees.

Today we are accustomed to the fact that mail bags are automatically dropped off and picked up as the fast Travelling Post Office races along the railways to some of the bigger towns.

It is, however, salutary to learn that a similar performance took place as the mail coach swung speedily past some of the post-houses. The drivers had orders that they were to stop only to change horses, and that they were not to stop at any place merely to exchange mail bags. The guards had to blow their horns to give postmasters notice of the coach's arrival so that they could be ready to exchange mail bags as the coach was passing through at speed.

The use of the mail coach speeded the delivery of letters very considerably, but it was the advent of the steam engine which really gave the postal service its biggest impetus. Letters were first sent by train in the year 1830. It was this which prepared the way for the reforms which Rowland Hill was to inaugurate ten years later.

Until this time, and for some time after the advent of the steam engine, no parcel post service was in operation. True, there are stories of some goods being sent by letter carrier. One concerns an order for a new hat to be sent from town to a man living in the country. The postman was told that he must wear the hat as the best way of getting it safely to its purchaser, but he was instructed to see that it was protected from rain. When the parcel post service did begin to operate it was soon found that the cost of sending parcels by train made it impractical and it was eventually arranged that the overnight coach should be reintroduced for this purpose. This was continued until motor vans came into use.

Horses were still used in rural districts, sometimes with carts or gigs. The postman's uniform was changed, and red piping on the trousers and facings became the accepted pattern. The new grey uniform of today, however, does not carry the traditional red piping.

Yet another twenty-five years passed before the first letter boxes began to appear in the larger towns; some were free standing and very ornate in design, others were built into walls. The first pillar box was erected in Jersey, and Anthony Trollope, the novelist, who was Surveyor in the Post Office at the time, is

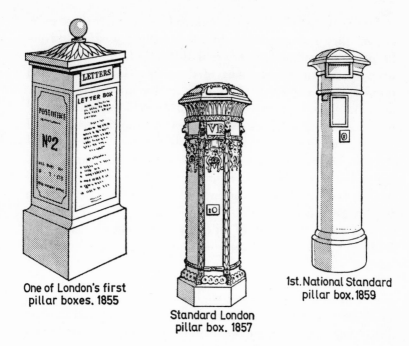

One of London's first
pillar boxes. 1855

Standard London
pillar box. 1857

1st. National Standard
pillar box. 1859

Some of the first pillar boxes were very ornate in design

thought to have been the man responsible. France had introduced them a few years earlier but many people regarded them
as unsafe, and continued to hand their letters to the clerk at the
post office. The emptying of these boxes became part of the
regular duty of the letter carriers, or postmen, as they now
began to be called. Today, except in isolated areas, there are
pillar boxes within walking distance of most people's homes; a
service which is taken very much for granted, as are the little
red vans which make collection and delivery so much easier
than in the past. Many older people can remember when these
vans were introduced, yet now, with sixty thousand vehicles
covering five hundred million miles a year, the Post Office is one
of the motor trade's biggest customers.

The vans are built in a Birmingham factory. After leaving the factory they are despatched to another plant used exclusively for post office vehicles. It is here that 'Royal Mail' transfers are fixed to the sides and doors of the vans. Here also, special requirements are attended to, such as fitments for vans to be used by engineers, while all post office vehicles have special locks fitted. Post Office inspectors are appointed to all factories which handle contracts, but before a contract is placed, contractors are required to have the vans tested for such things as hill climbing, fuel consumption and manoeuvrability. For this purpose the Post Office has its own testing ground.

With many thousands of miles a year travelled by each van, its average life varies between five and thirteen years, according to its size.

Planning the van routes to the best advantage has been quite a headache for the officials concerned, but London's central fleet is now controlled by computer. Thirty thousand trips are made each week between the main London railway stations and the district sorting offices. The computer does not tell the drivers which route to take, but it does work out the order of calls, enabling a van delivering mail at one point to go on and collect more at another, without returning to base in between. It reduces empty running time as well as waiting periods, though it does not overlook the drivers' rest and meal breaks, even telling him where to find the nearest post office canteen. Since the vans operate twenty-four hours a day, the programme has to make allowances for rush hours and night journeys. But traffic hold-ups can throw out any schedule, however carefully planned, and while admitting the computer planned journeys have their good points, some drivers claim that they now finish their last journey much later than formerly. Doubtless improvements to the programming will be made in the light of further experience and, if this experiment proves successful, it may be extended to journeys from other large towns. Whatever is done, the economical organizing of the running of the largest fleet of commercial vehicles in the country can never be a simple matter.

To make full use of these vans in outlying areas without adequate transport facilities, the postal authorities decided, in 1967, to run a series of six rural mail bus experiments. The routes were chosen jointly by the Post Office and the Ministry of Transport, after consultation with local authorities and others concerned. Experimental services were introduced in Montgomeryshire, the Lake District, Devon and East Lothian. Between them they carry five to six thousand passengers a year; this in places where a service was needed, and where it fits in with postal operating requirements. More routes will be added as investigations reveal the need and practicability of such services.

5

Sorting the Mail

With the ever increasing volume of mail posted and delivered each day, the problems of efficient and speedy sorting are constantly under research and review.

Business houses tend to despatch most, if not all, of their mail by the late afternoon or early evening post, as indeed do a vast number of individuals. This results in a massive amount of work at the various sorting offices during the latter part of the day. Whether it be a district or central sorting office, the task of handling this huge quantity of letters, packets and parcels must be executed with the utmost speed in order that the sorted and bagged mail may reach the various railway stations in time to catch specified trains.

From Monday to Friday the main time for collection of mail is between a quarter to six and half past. On these evenings there is increasing pressure on sorting staff in all offices as the contents of the postmen's bags are emptied onto the tables for sorting to begin. This involves many different operations, even at district level. First there is the need to segregate first class from second class mail. Then the different packets sent by letter post must be separated from the ordinary letters and cards. It is important that this is done because such packets cannot be put through the stamp cancelling machine with the letters, but must be handled separately. Except in those sorting offices in large towns where segregating machines have been installed, large envelopes must be hand-sorted from smaller ones. Before these can be put through the stamp cancelling machine which, in most offices, is mechanically operated, they must be 'faced', which simply means stacking them so that the stamps are all in the same position, facing the same way.

The stamp cancelling machine not only does what its name suggests but, in the same operation, stamps the date and place on each letter as it passes swiftly through at the rate of seven hundred letters each minute. It also counts the letters as they pass through. Wooden frames are fixed down the room, each with forty-eight pigeon-holes. Every one of these holes is marked with the town, county or group of counties, depending on whether sorting is being done at a district or central office. Postmen sorters stand ready at each frame to sort the letters into the appropriate pigeon-holes as quickly as an expert deals a pack of cards. The divisions, all within arm's reach, are so familiar to them that they hardly need to look at the name on the frame. Delays occur when a letter is not clearly addressed. This may have to be put aside to be checked and deciphered later. These letters often have to be despatched with a query as to which county or town they are intended for. It is to avoid delays of this kind that postal authorities ask for names of towns to be written or printed clearly in block letters, followed by the name of the county in small letters.

Another chore for the sorting office staff is the redirection of letters, whether in the case of permanent or temporary change of address. This is done at the addressee's local sorting office, and is a service performed free of charge for the first three months, five shillings for the next twelve months and ten shillings for each subsequent year.

Sorting is a tiring business, with work going on against the clock. As one batch of letters begins to lessen another batch is added to the sorters' table, while, on the other side, postmen remove those that are sorted. At the end of the sorting stands, empty mail bags hang open on their iron frames ready to receive the bundles of mail as they are tied up for the various places to which they are to be despatched. There are separate bags for different areas in this country, as well as those for overseas and for ships at sea.

Depending on their destination the mail bags go either to the district office for final sorting, or to a central office which acts as a distributing centre.

The biggest central office is that at Mount Pleasant, in central London, once a debtors' prison. It claims to be one of the biggest offices of its kind in the world. Here, in a building covering an area of nine acres, a staff of between six and seven thousand handle the mail which arrives in fifty thousand mail bags every day. This comes from all over the country and from overseas, to be sorted for inland delivery. It is estimated that one out of every eight letters posted in this country comes to this office for sorting.

In the section dealing with overseas mail, there is a Customs table where selected packets are opened to assess duty chargeable. Mail arriving in this country by boat is dealt with at the town of arrival. Such mail is transported in coarse hessian bags, while that travelling by air is packed in strong nylon bags. Letters and bags which are damaged are put in a basket and dealt with later. Football pool mail is all put into one box.

A bill is made out showing the number of special items, such as registered or insured packets. Men work in much the same way as in smaller offices, sorting the letters for size and area and putting the parcels in baskets under the sorting tables for special treatment elsewhere in the building. The task here is to get this mass of mail into some sort of order before sending it nearer to its destination.

The investigation branch is responsible for withholding pornographic literature, drugs and other unlawful packages.

Into Mount Pleasant sorting office alone come three thousand badly addressed letters and packets each day, business people being the worst offenders. As in all other offices, this incurs delay in despatch.

A roadway and loading platforms separate the two main sorting floors—one for letters, packets and newspapers, the other for parcels.

The fifteen facing machines in the letter sorting office count and stamp letters at the rate of six hundred a minute before they are passed on to the sorters. The frames in the preliminary sorting section cover wide geographical areas which are sub-divided when the mail reaches the second sorting tables. Mail bags are delivered at the eastern end of the building. When ready for despatch, the sorted and re-bagged mail is taken to loading platforms at the western end of the building, where fleets of vans are waiting to take it to railway stations or all the way by road. At the local office it is again sorted into different parts of the town or postal district. Even at that point there has to be a second sorting to subdivide the mail into the postmen's walks.

Meanwhile the awkward packets or different sized letters are dealt with elsewhere. Stamp cancelling of these is done by hand, and sorting is done on a horizontal grid of named containers, with trap doors beneath the containers which release the contents to conveyor belts below. This is a very ingenious machine, known familiarly by the staff as the 'submarine'. Trap doors open one at a time every three minutes, while a deflector arm moves across to direct the packages into the correct chute, thus keeping the sorted mail still segregated one county from another as it goes on for its second and more detailed sorting before being bagged and loaded for despatch with the rest of the mail. Newspapers, magazines and other second class mail is dealt with in off-peak periods of sorting.

In the parcel section the staff handle more than a million parcels each week. These include those routed through London from the provinces, as well as those collected from business houses and post offices in the London area. The bags are taken from the eastern arrival platforms and the contents tipped into hoppers, and conveyed to an endless belt which moves them along the top of a huge parcel ramp, known as a *glacis*. This is like a big table, one hundred and forty feet long, and built in a sloping position so that the parcels are carried down by gravity for preliminary sorting. Remote control ploughs, or deflectors, distribute the parcels evenly over the ramp. Men with sets of baskets on trolleys, each bearing the name of different areas or counties, sort these parcels by hand before they are moved on for their second sorting, followed by bagging, sealing and labelling. The bags are then taken by conveyor belt to the western end of the building for despatch by van or railway. By the mid 1970's parcel sorting will be concentrated in thirty-four highly mechanized centres, each serving a large surrounding area.

Foreign parcels are not handled at Mount Pleasant, but are taken to the Royal Agricultural Hall for sorting. This has been used for foreign parcels ever since fire bombs partially destroyed the main parcels office at Mount Pleasant during the Second World War. Now the Royal Agricultural Hall is the largest parcels office in the country and is responsible for sorting the half million parcels which are despatched every month all over the world, 15 per cent going by air. This airlift for parcels—the first in the world—was introduced in 1921. It now covers a network of about one hundred and eighty countries, with about two and a quarter million parcels flown out of this country and approximately one million a year coming into the country.

One section of Mount Pleasant is known as 'heartbreak corner'. Here, parcels which are not properly tied, or which are carelessly protected from breakages, are dealt with. Thousands of badly packed parcels have to be repacked. Sometimes bottles with liquid contents become broken in transit, making other parcels wet or sticky. In one sorting office an odd buzzing noise occurred while sorting was being done. Investigation showed that this came from bees in a mail bag. Experts called in to deal with them found that two worker bees, sent as travelling companions for six queen bees, had escaped from their package. The worker bees were removed and the queen bees properly repacked.

It is for reasons such as this that the Post Office lays down specific rules in the *Post Office Guide* about the correct method of packing such parcels. There are many occasions when, because of insecure or poor quality wrapping, it is impossible to know to whom the parcel was addressed, or to discover the name and address of the sender. In such cases, if the contents are not claimed within a specified period, they are sold by auction.

The largest 'Dead Letter Office' in the country used to be at Mount Pleasant. This office dealt with property lost in the post; or mail which, for various reasons, could neither be delivered nor returned to sender. It also dealt with enquiries and claims concerning missing mail, endeavouring to connect the enquiries with the actual items referred to.

To give badly needed space for mechanization at Mount Pleasant, the 'Dead Letter Office' or 'Returned Letter Branch' was moved to Portsmouth in January 1968. This office at Portsmouth now does the work for the whole of London, South Eastern and Eastern Postal Regions, which represents about a third of all the 'dead letter' work in this country.

There are many ways in which the Post Office makes possible special delivery of letters and packets. Railway and airway letters and parcels are two of these. Anyone may take a letter or package to a railway station or airport and ask for it to be put on the next available train or direct air service to the nearest point of destination. Arrangements can be made either for it to be collected at the receiving station or airport, or posted from there to the addressee. Normal postage must be prepaid as well as an additional fee.

On receipt of a telephone request express messengers will convey urgent letters or goods all the way from the sender to the recipient. This service only operates if staff is available during normal business hours at all London and provincial post offices which have a delivery of telegrams. It is not available on Sundays or on some specified public holidays. Charges vary according to distance and means of conveyance. In addition to the normal charge for the service, a waiting charge is payable should the messenger have to wait for a reply.

These services are restricted to first class mail.

Letters and parcels may be sent to an addressee at any post office except a town sub-office. The words 'To Be Called For', or 'Poste Restante', should be written on the envelope between the name of the addressee and the particular post office. Those who call for such letters must furnish evidence of identity. This is a service provided for the convenience of travellers.

While, in general, postmen are not allowed to carry private packages, they may, in rural districts, carry medicine sent by a doctor or chemist to a patient. In special cases they may also carry newspapers from a publisher to a newsagent in a rural area.

Many specified articles for the blind, including braille books, may be sent free of postage provided no letter is enclosed, and if they comply with certain conditions which are set out in the *Post Office Guide*.

Every day, ships carry mail to all parts of the world, while air services carry it on practically all their fastest journeys. Special air mail stamps are not necessary on mail addressed to European countries. It will be despatched by air automatically if this provides the quickest route. So popular has this become that over a million letters and parcels are sent overseas from this country every day.

The Forces postal service is another big part of the work of the Post Office. Operated by servicemen of the Royal Engineers courier and postal service, it links servicemen with their relatives. Every year fifty million letters and a million parcels are despatched to overseas forces, and about the same number are received in this country.

The cost of transporting mail by all services represents about 16 per cent of the total annual expenditure of the postal services.

Following the introduction of the two-tier postal system, in

September 1968, delivery next day will generally be made only for letters bearing a fivepenny stamp. Those with a fourpenny stamp will normally take a day longer to be delivered. Printed papers, which formerly went in open envelopes with a three-penny stamp, may now be sealed and sent either first class or second class, according to the speed of service required by the poster. Similarly, old newspapers may be sent by either service. New newspapers may be paid for at the second class rate but are given first class treatment.

The two-tier postage system was introduced to spread the work at the sorting offices. With the ever growing number of staff required to deal with an increasing volume of work, and the rise in rates of pay over the years, wages now account for three-quarters of the cost of the services, far too high a figure for economic efficiency. By charging more for speedy delivery, a much smaller amount of mail has to be sorted in the evening, while the sorting of that bearing a fourpenny stamp can be spread over off-peak periods, with a consequent economy in time and money.

Until the two-tier sorting system was introduced, the public were able to anticipate, with a certain amount of confidence, that all inland letters bearing a fourpenny stamp would be delivered to their respective addresses on the day after posting. Though complaints were made at the failures, the number of letters which, for one reason or another, did not reach their destination in this country the next day was very small compared with the thirty-five million letters posted every day. Two-thirds of these thirty-five million letters, posted mostly in the early evening, have to be sorted and despatched in time for delivery to the eighteen million homes and business houses early the next day. Letters can pass through as many as three or four sorting offices, and travel for hundreds of miles by van and rail-way to a tight timetable, before reaching their final sorting and delivery.

With its eighteen million delivery points, the Post Office delivers, in proportion to population, to more individuals, homes and offices than does any other country in the world. Few, if any, business organizations can provide a service which is 100 per cent satisfactory, and the Post Office reliability for a 94 per cent next-day delivery service of first class mail is the envy of the world.

In 1965 the Post Office Consultancy Service was set up. Its purpose is to put at the disposal of overseas administrations the years of experience of the British Post Office in the planning and mechanization of new sorting offices. It has planned mechanization schemes in Tehran, Oslo and Jamaica, to name only a few. A charge is made for this service, based on costs incurred.

Postage has gone up only from three halfpence to fivepence (for some items) in thirty years. Wages show at least as high a percentage rise in the same period.

Yet the increased rates, and the two-tier sorting and delivery, caused a storm of protests. This was due, in part, to the unfortunate publicity campaign announcing the change. Had the announcement of increased postage been made with a clear statement of the reason for this, there would doubtless have been a certain amount of complaint, but since economic conditions have resulted in rising prices of most services, it would have occasioned no more protest than did the rise in railway or bus fares. Even with these new rates, Britain's minimum postage is lower than any country in Europe, with the exception of Spain, where the postal service is less efficient.

In the same way, if two-tier sorting and delivery had been clearly attributed to the need to overcome the problems associated with the ever increasing volume of letters collected and sorted in the early evening, there would have been far less controversy, for this is a problem which besets every country in the world.

Of course there were bound to be teething troubles. Any new system must go through a trial period. The Postmaster General stated, in a Parliamentary debate on the subject, that 'it was obvious that this dramatic change in the way the Post Office did its business would have to be subject to review'. For that reason one of the postal regional directors was asked to conduct a full-scale survey of its operation.

It would appear, however, that no better alternative method of dealing with the problems is likely to be found.

6

Post Office Trains

Not all the mail sorted at Mount Pleasant and other central offices goes to the railway station by van. Some goes along conveyor belts and down spiral chutes or lifts to London's Post Office Railway, seventy feet below ground. This underground railway is unique in that it carries no passengers and does not require drivers or guards; in fact staff are not allowed to travel on it. Completely automatic, it has a record for safety second to none.

As long ago as 1853 Rowland Hill said mail ought to be carried underground, but his suggestion was met with incredulity and ridicule. In spite of this a pneumatic tube system was tried out, though this was abandoned after two years because of technical problems. A more ambitious scheme was drawn up in 1910, but the First World War delayed its development. During the war the tunnels which had been made were used as shelters and as places for the nation's art treasures. American engineers, who later inspected the tunnels, were sceptical after their failure with a similar project in Chicago. In spite of this, work proceeded until the railway was finally completed in 1927, and the first fully automatic and remote-controlled underground railway began to operate: a triumph for British engineers after the opposition they had encountered. The intention was to speed the mail by avoiding the congested streets between seven large

sorting offices and the main London railway termini at Paddington and Liverpool Street.

Troubles abounded during the early years and technicians
were on call for twenty-four hours a day. Cars were redesigned
to give a larger capacity for mail and to avoid difficulties on
curves due to the long wheelbase.

In this, as in all else, the railway has been entirely successful.
It takes one hour and ten minutes for each of the trains to make
the double journey on the six and a half mile track, from
Paddington to the Eastern District office at Whitechapel,
stopping at Liverpool Street and each of the sorting offices.
These underground trains cover about thirty thousand car
miles per week. Thousands of letter and parcel bags are moved
by this means every day, a train being loaded every two
minutes during peak periods. There are sixty cars but these are
never all in use at one time. While some are being serviced,
others are held in strategic positions in loops, sidings and
'through' roads to meet conditions not fully catered for
by the standard timetable. Many of the cars are connected together to form two car trains in order to increase the carrying
capacity.

In appearance this railway is similar to the normal passenger
underground railways, except that the platforms have no
waiting passengers and the walls contain no advertisements.
Gradients of one in twenty on either side of each station assist
acceleration and deceleration. Lower voltages are used to give
reduced speed in the station areas.

Trains run at thirty-five miles an hour through a single
tunnel, and automatically slow down to eight miles an hour as
the tunnel divides into two. Most tunnels are seven feet in
diameter at the station approaches, while the departure
tunnels are larger. The track between any two stations is divided
into automatic sections for train control purposes, while movements in the station areas are governed by a control panel at the
station. At five of the station control points, a switchman gives
constant attention to a lever frame in order to maintain the

service to a timetable. At some of the smaller stations the route through the station is pre-set, and the trains re-start automatically when the 'train ready' signal is given by the platform staff.

The train itself is electrically driven and can be run with one or two cars, each twenty-seven feet in length. A car is composed of a body slung between two motored bogies. Each body holds four containers which are filled on the station platform before being wheeled onto the trains. One hundred and twenty letter bags, or forty-eight parcel bags, can be carried on each train, though they are not all loaded at one station. Altogether forty thousand mail bags are carried by this means every day of the year, with many more at the Christmas period.

Movement of mail to and from stations is swift and, as far as possible, mechanical, with man-handling reduced to a minimum. Apertures on the platforms of the main line railway stations at Liverpool Street and Paddington give access to chutes and conveyors on which the mail is carried to the Post Office underground station. On the platform this is loaded into containers. Numbered destination labels, corresponding with the station number, are clipped to the containers as required—white labels being used for letters and blue for parcels. Trains follow one another into the station at short intervals, so there is no chance of the platforms becoming congested with mail bags or waiting containers.

A push button, connected with the control room, indicates to the operator that the train is loaded ready to move, and away it goes with no further manual work.

On arrival at the next station the appropriate containers are removed and replaced by others. In less than two minutes the station controller despatches the driverless train, while the containers which have been removed from the train are wheeled into lifts. Where stations have under-platform conveyors, each container is wheeled onto a mechanized tipper which empties it, discharging the bags onto conveyors.

The same thing happens in reverse for outgoing mail which

leaves the six sorting offices for despatch from the two main line stations. In the Western District Office an ingenious method of transporting parcel bags from the sorting office has been achieved by the use of chain conveyors containing a number of hooks. When the bags are sealed ready for despatch, with destination labels attached, they are hooked onto the conveyor. Each hook has a lever which is set to correspond with its particular chute, for delivery east or west, and gravity does the rest.

In the control room the traffic controller is connected by a separate automatic telephone system to the individual stations and to the maintenance engineers. The position of each train in the system is indicated on an illuminated track diagram in one or other of the station control rooms. This indicates that a train is occupying a particular section of track. The switchman records the movements of each train.

Trains run continuously throughout the day from ten o'clock on Monday mornings until eight o'clock on Sunday mornings, with only a two-hour break from eight to ten o'clock each morning.

The busy maintenance centre, where work continues for twenty-four hours a day, is in the basement of Mount Pleasant sorting office. This is connected with the railway by a steep two-track tunnel. Routine adjustments are made after every two and a half thousand miles, and a complete overhaul after each eighty thousand miles. Each of the sixty cars has covered about one and a half million miles.

Although the Post Office Railway did not come into being until nine years after the conclusion of the First World War, postal sorting on trains has been carried on in one way or another since 1838. In that year a horse box was fitted up as a sorting office, on the Grand Junction Railway, operating between Birmingham and Liverpool. It proved so successful that soon the Travelling Post Office became part of the postal service. Now it carries mail from one end of the country to the other; in fact, every town in the country receives mail from the overnight postal railway service. One-third of the traffic handled by the Travelling Post Office is done by four special trains travelling to and from the north and west of the country. Known as the 'Up Special' and the 'Down Special', and the 'Great Western Up' and 'Great Western Down', they have a maximum speed of eighty miles an hour from Euston as far as Glasgow and Aberdeen, and from Paddington to Penzance, while two others make the journey in the reverse direction, each of them picking up more and more mail *en route*. The rule that no passengers may be carried is strictly adhered to, especially since the Great Train Robbery of 1963, when over two and a half million pounds was stolen from the 'Up Special' in one of the most daring raids ever carried out.

Prior to the introduction of the two-tier postal service, a total of about six hundred million different items were sorted on T.P.O.'s throughout the year. Special coaches on which mail is carried and sorted during the journey are attached to many fast overnight passenger trains. Some of these connect with one of the four specials; some are attached to the specials at certain junctions.

The timing of all T.P.O. trains which carry mail is subject to the convenience of the Post Office, in fact the railway and postal authorities work very closely together. The four 'T.P.O. Specials', or Travelling Post Office Specials, are not listed in any passenger timetable and are seldom seen by the public unless they wish to post a letter, or happen to be around at the time the trains leave. For a small additional fee, first class mail can be posted in the trains' late fee boxes up to the time of departure, which, in the case of the Great Western T.P.O. Down, is as late as ten-twenty at night. A letter box is let into the side of one of the coaches for this purpose.

T.P.O. coaches are painted in the BR Rail Blue/Rail Grey livery, with the words ROYAL MAIL painted on the side in white letters, together with the royal insignia—E II R. The Up Special T.P.O. has seven sorting coaches and five stowage vans. The sorting carriages are sixty-three feet long and are specially built for the Post Office, with frames of pigeon-holes and hooks for the mail bags. Some of the carriages have special facilities for releasing and taking on mail while the train is still in motion.

Work starts long before the trains leave their respective stations. First the mail bags have to be loaded onto the train. These may have come from the Post Office underground railway in the case of the Great Western T.P.O. Down, or direct from a sorting office not served by the railway. Mail which has already been sorted for a particular town is loaded into the stowage carriages. There is an ordered routine about this. That which has to be dropped off while the train is in motion must be placed so that it is easily accessible to the special apparatus for disposing of it.

More than an hour before the train is timed to depart, post office staff are busy dealing with the first bags of mail in the sorting carriages. Speed in sorting and handling mail is of prime importance on these journeys since all the mail for the first stop must be sorted, bundled, bagged and sealed by the time the train arrives at the station. Some of the mail has to be taken off while the train is in transit. This mail, when sorted, is bagged and strapped in strong leather pouches. Post Office officials working on the train know precisely when the time comes to drop one lot of bags and pick up others. To a man trained to this work a change of sound, such as that made when the train passes under a bridge, or over a level crossing, may be sufficient indication that the doors of the carriage must be slid back into their recess, and the supporting arms to which the suspension straps of the leather pouches are attached must be operated.

Split second timing and absolute accuracy are essential. On the side of the track a rope net is attached to a supporting structure of wooden posts and a hinged iron frame. When the net is open to receive mail, a flexible steel cable is stretched across the front of it. As the train rushes by at up to eighty miles an hour, the leather suspension straps to which the mail bags are attached, and which have been swung out and suspended over the line, hit the steel cable with such force that the bags are released and thrown into the net. At the same time another net is swung out from the train, which snatches the pouches hanging from a cast iron standard by the side of the line, and throws them in at the open door of the carriage. They fall on the floor of the sorting carriages with such force that a bell is rung while this operation is in progress, to warn staff to keep clear of the area.

This method of disposing and collecting mail has been in operation for the whole of the time that the T.P.O. trains have been running.

All through the night these trains continue their journey, sometimes releasing men from their onerous duties and taking on fresh staff while exchanging mail bags at different points. At certain stations other trains wait to take the mail away in different directions. At others, additional mail trains are hitched on to the T.P.O., each with its quota of sorting to do for its particular towns.

The staff employed on this work are very experienced and must be physically fit. They have to be able to stand up to the strain of working to a strict timetable for long hours, when a mistake could be serious for the safe conduct of the mail. Staff who leave the train part way through its journey either travel back to the starting point on a T.P.O. going in the reverse direction, or, in the case of the Down Special, travel to Carlisle and return to London the following night.

The Down Special T.P.O. arrives at its final destination about eight o'clock in the morning; the other 'specials' arrive much earlier depending on the length of their journey. The total distance travelled by these trains every night is about seventeen hundred miles.

The mail bags remaining at the end of the journey, as all those deposited in the course of the night, are despatched by mail vans to the respective sorting offices in the town around the station, for the final sorting into postmen's walks, and delivery is achieved at most places by first post that morning. Though this service to the public has become regular and dependable, its satisfactory achievement is no small tribute to those who first organized the night mails and to those who have carried it on since. The whole thing is dependent on a loyal and efficient staff.

Burlington Arcade: 150
YEARS OF PUBLIC SERVICE
1819 – 1969

7

Automation in the Post Office

In a publication put out by the Post Office within the last twenty years, this comment on the subject of mechanization was made:

'When one considers the variety of addresses, the range of mail service from a centre such as London, and the mixture of size and shape of postal packets, it appears highly improbable that much more could be done to mechanize the postal service.'

Yet the G.P.O. Research Department is always planning and carrying out experiments towards this end. Only a few years after the comment was published, two machines were developed which are already proving themselves invaluable in the sorting of mail, while today such great advances in mechanization have been made that the possibilities of full mechanization seem very bright, especially in view of the fact that the Post Office plans to spend thirty-eight million pounds on postal plant during the five year period 1968-9 to 1972-3.

So much has to be considered when carrying out research tests on possible new machines that it is years before they can be put into effective use. Machinery of this kind is so costly that exhaustive tests must be made to prove that it will get the work done more cheaply and efficiently.

When the Post Office Research Station has made its tests there is the question of cost to be considered. The cost of installing such machines in the larger sorting offices alone is so enormous that, before money is invested in them, it must be clearly demonstrated that they will stand up to all the things demanded of them both now and in the future.

For this reason such machines are put on trial in a busy sorting office for a period of years. This brings to light the disadvantages as well as the advantages, and enables adjustments or modifications to be made to the machines so that they will function satisfactorily for the particular job they have to do. It also gives some indication as to whether they will, in time, justify the expense of installing them, and to what extent.

A great many alterations have to be made to the selected office itself in order to accommodate all the machines required. This, of course, is another reason why it is so important that detailed and continuous testing must be done before automation is adopted generally. Many sorting offices are in need of modernization and extension. New offices are to be built as part of the five year plan, and the requirements of new and faster means of sorting must be borne in mind in the planning of these if, for instance, wooden pigeon-holes are to be replaced by an Electronic Letter Sorter, to mention only part of the scheme.

Norwich was the office chosen for the experiment with coding and automatic letter sorting. The machines installed there use some of the most advanced techniques in the world, and the experiment has been so successful that the system has been extended to other towns.

By the end of 1968, as a preliminary to the mechanization of letter sorting, postcodes had been introduced in thirty-seven provincial towns and their neighbouring areas, and in the London W.1. postal district. It is anticipated that, by 1970, the whole of London and the remaining seventy or so major provincial towns will have been coded. Postcodes are a condensed form of address which can be transcribed by an operator into a pattern of phosphorescent dots on an envelope. The new sorting machines, such as those at Norwich and other towns, interpret the pattern and automatically sort the letters at high speed at all stages of their journey. This effects a saving of several manual sortings.

To obtain the full benefits of this it is essential that the towns to which the letters are addressed should have the code written in following the name of the town. This cannot work effectively until *all* towns are given a postcode and the public remember to use it.

In the modern sorting office large machines dominate the scene. First there is the Segregator, which separates letters from

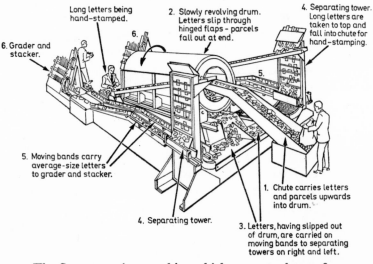

The Segregator is a machine which separates letters from packets

packets. As the mail comes into the office it is emptied into a hopper which feeds it into an inclined rotating drum in which are a series of hinged flaps. Bulky mail passes over these flaps and goes straight through the drum to the lower end, where it is hand-stamped. Letters, however, slip between the flaps and are carried along by conveyor belt into stacking devices. These have a series of rollers with gaps across which the shorter letters cannot pass and can be stacked separately at the bottom of the machine. Envelopes which are longer, bridge over the gaps and travel on to the top of the stacker. Twenty-five thousand items an hour are dealt with in this way.

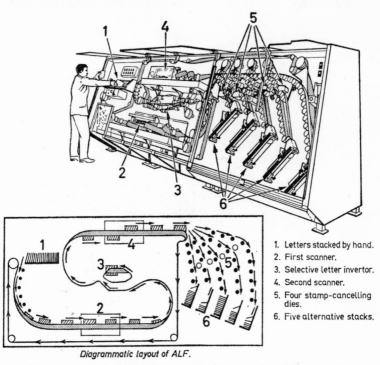

Diagrammatic layout of ALF.

1. Letters stacked by hand.
2. First scanner.
3. Selective letter invertor.
4. Second scanner.
5. Four stamp-cancelling dies.
6. Five alternative stacks.

The Automatic Letter Facer turns letters the right way for cancellation and sorting

Packets still have to be hand-stamped, but the remainder of the mail goes on to an Automatic Letter Facer (ALF). All stamps now issued in this country have phosphorescent bars. The fourpenny stamp has a single bar. All other stamps have two bars. The Automatic Letter Facer is a machine which picks out the phosphor bars to turn all letters the right way round and right way up ready for cancellation and sorting. In doing this the machine can partially sort by separating the letters with a single bar (fourpenny stamp) from all others. The remainder of the sorting is done by hand. A stamp cancelling printing die is incorporated so that when the letters are extracted from the machine they are ready for coded sorting. All this is done

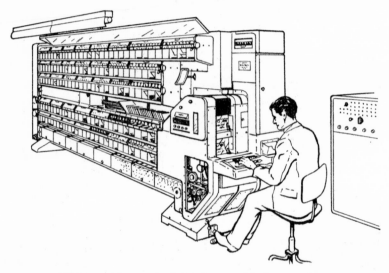

This machine sorts eight thousand letters an hour

automatically at the rate of over twenty thousand items an hour, a very great deal more quickly than could be done by hand.

Letters have to be fed into each coding desk output stack manually, but eventually they will be fed automatically.

A postman sits in front of a small keyboard. As the letters are fed out of the stack one at a time into the operator's line of vision, he depresses certain keys and so copies the letters and figures comprising the code. This transposes the code into two lines of phosphorescent dots, which are printed on the envelope, one above and one below the address.

The letters are now ready for the Automatic Letter Sorting Machine. This machine reads the bottom line of dots in order to sort the letters to destination towns, directing them to one of the one hundred and forty-four stacking boxes which are part of the machine, and are each labelled with a different destination. The controlling equipment which does this is the 'brain' of the whole thing and is made up of a large number of mechanical and electronic devices. The advantages of this machine are obvious, for not only can letters be sorted at a much greater speed than formerly (the machine sorts at the rate of eight thousand letters an hour) but also they are broken down to three times as many places. One hundred and forty-four stacking boxes replace the forty-eight pigeon-holes used in hand-sorting. Thus, with one operation in this machine, letters are ready for despatch to their office of destination. There are other machines which read the upper line of dots and so sort the letters into streets ready for the postmen's walks.

It is to enable more mail to be put through these electronic machines that post office preferred envelopes have been introduced. Plenty of variety in size is permissible, both in small and larger oblong envelopes, but they need to be kept within the specified range of sizes and weight of paper laid down, if they are all to receive the same speedy electronic treatment in sorting. It is also partly because open envelopes tend to get caught in the machines that second class mail may now be sealed.

No other organization deals, as the Post Office does at the Christmas season, with every member of every household. Yet, in spite of this terrific volume of additional mail, it is all delivered in time. Immediately one Christmas season finishes, planning begins for the next. Post mortems are held on the one which has just passed and, in the light of experience, plans are laid. From September a small staff is appointed to deal with the problems of storage, transport and recruitment of the additional people who will be needed in increasing numbers as the season advances. By the late autumn, in the London

postal region alone, the volume of letters begins to increase
from the normal twelve million a day to a peak of thirty-three
million, while parcel post doubles in volume. To cope with this,
temporary offices are taken over and, in some areas, temporary
buildings are erected.

So the work of the Post Office goes on, with amazing regu-
larity, day after day, week after week and month after month
all through the year. When strikes or 'go slow' affect the railways the mail still goes through by road or whatever means are
available, with only slight delays. When floods occur, with
railways and roads out of use, mail is switched to higher roads
unaffected by flooding. Just as, in the days of the mail coach,
drivers and guards traversed bad roads and braved attacks by
highwaymen, so the men and women employed in the service
of the post today have a sense of loyalty and a determination
that the post shall go through no matter what the difficulties.

For forty years, until he retired at the age of seventy-two, an
Irish postman delivered the mail by bicycle over a twenty-two-
mile route, to places which seemed like the last outposts of
civilization, and his story is typical of others. Tales of loyalty
and endurance are told of many postmen and postwomen. One
postwoman carried her postbag regularly for fifty-one years,
only missing her delivery on four days during the whole period
of service. For more than three centuries packet boats have
crossed the Irish Sea in the service of the post. Orders which
were issued by the postal authorities to the commanders of
these boats were:

'You must run when you can, you must fight when you can
no longer run, and when you can fight no more you must sink
the mails before you strike.'

This kind of loyalty and endurance which has been instilled
into those in the service of the post over the years has made
possible the regular delivery of mail which we enjoy today.

A sectional drawing of the interior of an automatic telephone exchange showing from bottom upwards: 1. Cable chamber, with cables coming in from the street (on left and right) and going up to 2. The main distribution frames connecting up with 3. The apparatus room

A small box of equipment is placed in the boot of the car for a car radiophone

An exchange operator deals with a call from a customer using the car radiophone

Loading cable for COMPAC on HMTS *Monarch*

Rigid type repeaters in the foredeck shelter, ready for laying

A repeater being passed over bow sheaves of HMTS *Monarch*. These repeaters have to be joined into the cable while it is being laid

The Post Office Tower in the centre of London

Television racks at
Museum Telephone
Exchange

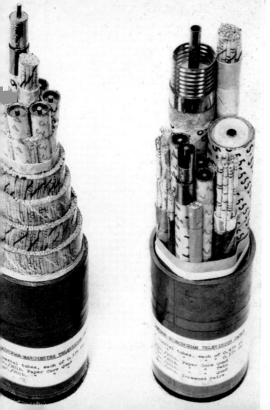

Television cables—
London–Birmingham and
Birmingham–Manchester

Rear of electronic clock in the Automatic Network Distribution Equipment at the London Television network switching centre

From the consoles in this Control Room the two operators control more than 100 vision and 150 sound circuits which terminate here, and also 400 BBC sound circuits

8

Telegraph, Teleprinters and Telex

Today it is possible for a telephone subscriber in this country to pick up a telephone receiver and be connected to almost any part of the world. By means of the teleprinter and the telex systems, a message can be printed as it is being typed in places as far away as Australia and New Zealand, while satellites launched over different parts of the world will result, in due course, in telephone and telex users being able to dial from every part of the world to every other part, at any time of the day or night.

The introduction and development of the railway system in this country were largely responsible for the introduction and growth of the telegraph and telephone service. With faster and greater means of travel came the need for faster and increasing numbers of messages to be sent.

Many outstanding men had experimented with different methods of communication, among them Michael Faraday. The son of a blacksmith, he discovered some of the secrets of electricity and its effects, one being that the movement of a magnet through a coil of wire causes an electric current to flow, a fact which is accepted as commonplace today, but which was great and astounding news then.

Yet it was not Faraday who was responsible for the first telegraph in this country. An inventor named Francis Ronalds, set up a system in his own garden on the outskirts of London. He laid eight miles of wire, putting it round and round his garden. At each end of the wire he fixed a dial which, when acted upon by the electric current which he created, caused a letter to appear before an opening. This was controlled by a pair of pith balls which were affected by an electric charge. It was a very crude affair as compared with later results, but it was a beginning. However, this was not recognized by the Government of the day when it was offered to them and it was left to others to bring the telegraph system successfully into being. The first practical telegraph in 1837 was the Euston Chalk Farm circuit in north-west London.

Many other famous men had a hand in making this possible: Morse, with the production of the alphabet in dots and dashes, known as the Morse Code; Edison, by his introduction of a system of increasing the capacity of a single wire; Lord Kelvin, whose experiments and discoveries prepared the way for the electric cable to be laid under the Atlantic by Charles Bright; and so to Marconi and his inventive brain which enabled messages to be sent across the sea without wires. Two of these men, Bright and Marconi, were only twenty-six years of age when they achieved their triumphs in this way.

For about thirty years the telegraph system was owned by private companies and railways; in fact, the first electric telegraph was used to signal the departure and arrival of trains from one station to another. After that period, inland telegraph communications were taken over by the postmaster general and specific rules were laid down about its almost exclusive control by the Post Office. The *Post Office Guide* defines the meaning of the term 'telegraph' as 'a wire or wires used for the purpose of telegraphic communications, whether worked by electricity or not, and any apparatus for transmitting messages or other communications by means of electric signals, whether involving the use of wires or not'.

In the early days the service was expensive, but under Post Office management it became so popular that before the end of the century it was possible to send a telegram of twelve words for sixpence. People even sent telegrams when they wanted clean handkerchiefs posted on to them! This was, of course, before the telephone became so widely used.

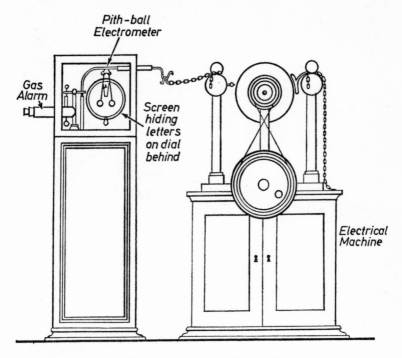

Francis Ronalds's telegraph

At the close of the last century ninety million telegrams were being handled annually by the Post Office. A special telegraph form had to be obtained at a post office or railway station, and the message clearly written by the sender ready for despatch by telegraphy. The usual procedure was that the post office clerk either tapped out the message on a morse code instrument, or used an instrument with a handle underneath which moved a

needle to and fro by long and short movements to represent the
morse code. These instruments were connected by electrical
lines to receiving sets in other offices many miles distant. The
clerk being called either listened to the sound of the tapped message or watched the movement of the needle at his end, and
wrote down the message for despatch by the telegraph boy.
Until after the First World War his mode of transport was an
ordinary push bike, with red frames and mudguards, or he went
on foot. Motor cycles were introduced between the wars. Often
these boys made considerable journeys with only a few telegrams,
for these were stamped at the receiving post office with the
date and time of receipt, and delays in despatch were not
contemplated.

With the increasing use of the telephone, private teleprinter
circuits and telex, the ordinary public telegraph service has
dwindled so much that even though the charge has increased
considerably, it is not paying its way. Its most general use now
is for social rather than business telegrams. Special greetings
forms are issued and used for birthdays, weddings and similar
events.

Not only is the price entirely different today, but so is the
method of despatch. Though telegrams can still be handed in
at the post office most people telephone the message to the
telegraph office in their area and the operator there types it
out on a teleprinter.

These machines are similar to an electric typewriter in that
they have a keyboard which is operated in much the same way
as a typewriter keyboard. It can either print the message on
paper, as an ordinary typewriter does, only with the advantage
that a similar machine at the receiving end simultaneously
prints the same copy; or it can print it on gummed tape. It is
this latter which is used in telegraph offices, the printed tape
being stuck onto a telegraph form. Both methods require an
operator at the sending end.

In London alone more than fifty operators may be employed
at one time to handle telegrams from private subscribers,

telephone call boxes, or those handed over the counter at small post offices. Delays of more than a few seconds in dealing with these are rare, but if an operator is not immediately available the message is held in a 'queue' until it can be dealt with.

This service also has private wires to special places, such as Buckingham Palace, Windsor Castle and the Weather Forecast Office. Besides sending out weather news this deals with flood and gale warnings.

Except in the case of overnight telegrams, which can be sent at half price, wherever possible the message is phoned to the recipient. The actual telegram is sent on by the next post, as are overnight telegrams. Alternatively they are sorted into 'walks' and delivered by messengers on motor cycles.

The overseas telegraph centre is at Electra House, London. Occupying one floor is an assembly of equipment known as the Overseas Tape Relay Unit (OTRU), with its peripheral equipment such as teleprinters. Overseas telegrams received in the unit in the form of punched paper tape are fed into an automatic transmitter and sent over a telegraph circuit to the country of destination. If the circuit is busy the messages are 'queued' to be sent automatically when the circuit is free.

Radio telegrams, replies to which may be prepaid, can be sent via Coast Stations in the United Kingdom, such as Portishead Radio, to merchant ships in any part of the world. If the sender does not know the name of the appropriate coast station, standard rate messages may be sent to Portishead Radio. The twelve coast radio stations situated around Britain's coasts are open twenty-four hours a day. This service was started in 1910. In 1928 a radio-telephone service was started which made communication possible with small ships not carrying a skilled telegraphist. This applies to ships up to sixteen hundred tons.

There is a specially reduced rate for radio telegrams sent to British trawlers, drifters and coastal vessels and ships plying regularly to and from certain ports of Europe, similarly to Her Majesty's ships.

Another method of message sending is by telex. By this means communications of all kinds can be exchanged with the speed of the telephone, and at the same time the authority of the printed word. Telex is better than a letter or telephone call when giving or receiving orders. An order placed by telephone has to be confirmed in writing, whereas it can be sent just as quickly by telex as by telephone, and has the advantage of providing a printed message for both parties at the sending and receiving end. Multi-ply paper can be used if six copies are required, or a stencil can be used if a large number of copies is needed. The equipment consists of a teleprinter and a dialling unit, with two lamps and four press buttons for operating control, and a dial. Telex subscribers have a number which is printed in a telex directory. They also have an 'answer-back' code which is an abbreviation of their name or business and town.

To make a call, a dial button is pressed which causes a green bulb to light, showing that the circuit is ready. The caller then dials the required number. When connected, the distant teleprinter automatically sends its 'answer-back' code so that the sender knows he is through to the correct number and he then sends his 'answer-back' code. The message is not spoken but typed on the teleprinter, and it is simultaneously received in typed form at the other end. When the message is completed the caller sends his 'answer-back' code and, by depressing a key marked 'who are you?', receives the code of the distant machine, which confirms that the whole of the message has been received. The call is disconnected from the exchange by pressing a button marked 'clear' on the dialling unit.

Incoming calls are indicated by the automatic lighting of the green lamps and the starting of the teleprinter motor. The 'answer-back' code is automatically transmitted to the caller. Provided the power is switched on, incoming calls can be received without attention at any time of the day or night.

This service began in 1954 with nine hundred subscribers. Today there are over twenty-four thousand. They can dial to eighteen countries; in fact, 93 per cent of overseas calls are dialled direct.

All outgoing and incoming international telex traffic, and all London inland telex traffic at present goes through Fleet Building's automatic switching equipment, with its fifteen hundred miles of wire. Fleet Building, in Farringdon Street, London E.C.4, is a modern fifteen-storey block for telecommunications and administration. On the administration side it houses services such as the North Central Telephone Manager's Office. This controls seventeen telephone exchanges which give access to two hundred and sixty-five thousand telephone instruments. It also controls a very large engineering and office staff, and a Sales Bureau where the latest equipment can be seen and the various facilities available to subscribers can be demonstrated.

Telecommunications are handled on the lower six floors, which were specially designed to accommodate the heavy equipment required.

A modern telex cordless switchboard has been installed and this is the only telex switchboard in the country. Operators on this board handle all the overseas calls which subscribers cannot dial for themselves. They also deal with enquiries and problems. To enable many different messages to be sent at the same time over one link, by cable or radio, transistorized equipment, known as a 'Multi-Channel Voice Frequency Modulator', has been installed. Because messages may be confused by atmospheric conditions when sent by radio, another piece of transistorized equipment has been installed to correct this. Known as 'Error Correction Equipment', its use enables the transmission of a message to be halted if a distorted code is received, and for that particular part of the message to be retransmitted. This happens automatically.

Since 1960, when automatic switching was introduced, subscribers have been able to dial most of their calls direct. Calls are charged in much the same way as telephone calls—in units of twopence, the amount of time charged per unit decreasing as the distance increases. On the whole, telex calls cost less than telephone calls of similar length.

Some large users rent their own cable or radio circuit from the Post Office. Outgoing inland calls alone average over one hundred and forty thousand a day, while the outgoing overseas calls number some fifty thousand a day on average. Traffic from the twenty-four thousand telex subscribers in this country to those overseas is greater than that from eight million telephones. There are telex subscribers in nearly every part of the world, and a vast and widespread volume of business is being achieved through this medium.

With the system expanding by 15–20 per cent every twelve months, there are formidable planning and operational problems.

9

Manual and Automatic Telephone Exchanges

There must be few people today who are not accustomed, to a greater or lesser degree, to using the telephone. For those who have no instrument in their own home there are the public call boxes in every post office, railway station and most stores, as well as in many streets, so that it is difficult to imagine a time when it did not exist.

Yet it was less than one hundred years ago, in 1875, that Alexander Graham Bell, a Scot who had emigrated to America, stumbled across the secret of the electrical transmission of speech. He was experimenting with something called the harmonic telegraph when he heard the voice of his assistant, who was in the next room adjusting a fault at the other end of the circuit. There was great excitement when Graham Bell realized that the voice was being transmitted through the circuit on which they were working.

A year later, in America, he produced the first telephone. It was made from pieces of clock springs and electro magnets. Shortly afterwards he brought it to England and demonstrated it to Queen Victoria. The idea quickly caught on and soon a number of telephone companies were established. Many of them tried to outdo the others in the elaborate design of their instruments, specimens of which can be seen in the Post Office Exhibition in Fleet House.

Everything did not go smoothly for the telephone service at first. The companies quarrelled among themselves and often fighting broke out on the roof tops of London houses. When one company ran a series of lines across the roof of a business house,

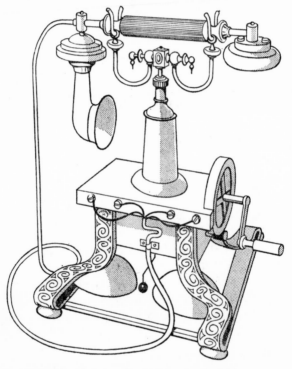

An early elaborately designed telephone

another came along and ran theirs across the others and so produced a tangle of wires. Endless squabbles arose, with saboteurs from one telephone company spiking the equipment of the other. They even went so far as to erect their telegraph poles in holes prepared by the other company for their own use. Two London companies fought it out in this way, often having recourse to police courts to settle their differences. Eventually the matter was resolved by one company taking over the other. This became the National Telephone Company.

In spite of the problems, the telephone became more and more popular, with telephone directories increasing in size all the time. Business men arranged to have the morning papers read over to them before they left for their offices. Some even had the telephone installed in their stables so that they could call their grooms when they needed their horses. At that time telephone exchanges were open only during business hours.

The first telephone operators were young boys who proved to be so mischievous that they were quickly replaced by girls. Shortly afterwards a night service was operated in Westminster for the use of Members of Parliament.

In 1912 the British Post Office paid five thousand pounds in a take-over of the independent companies, and so became practically the sole controller of the telephone network in this country. (The city of Hull is an exception. It still has its own municipal telephone service.) At that time there were only seven hundred thousand telephones in use. Today there are about ten million. For many years the instruments were all in black enamel, though there were the few exceptions such as the one produced in 1890, which is on show at the Telecommunications Exhibition in Fleet Building, and which was gold-plated. This was one used with a private switchboard owned by Lord Rothschild. Now, however, for a small initial payment, it is possible to obtain instruments in a variety of colours. The design of the telephone has changed, too, the latest being one known as 'trimphone', which weighs only two pounds, with the lightweight receiver resting on the instrument from front to back.

One of the many developments which are advantageous to private subscribers is the plug-in telephone which can be taken from room to room and plugged in. This is even more useful in hospitals and nursing homes, enabling patients to make calls while they are bedridden. A great deal of Post Office apparatus is designed to help the handicapped. This includes an amplifying telephone handset for the hard of hearing, a marked dial for the blind, a faint-speech amplifier for people with partial loss of voice and a sensitive button device enabling the disabled to contact the operator for assistance in making a call.

Basically, however, the telephone works in much the same way as when Graham Bell first invented it, consisting of a mouthpiece which holds a microphone, and an earpiece with a receiver. These are now in one holder known as the hand set. When the hand set is not in use it rests on the transmitter, the weight cutting off the electric current which runs through a pair of wires and out of the house through an underground pipe straight to a distribution box in the pavement. In some areas the wires which connect the telephone to the exchange still follow the overhead pole routes. These go out from the house to a distribution pole. They are then enclosed in a cable with several other pairs of wires from different houses, and the cable runs down the pole to the distribution box in the pavement. Here they meet more wires coming from other subscribers' telephones, and the whole bunch runs along to form a still larger cable which goes on to the telephone exchange. The fluctuating electric current is converted into sound waves as it passes into the receiver, or earpiece of the operator at the telephone switchboard.

The preparation and erection of telegraph poles is just one small part of the work which makes possible the use of our telephones.

Every year the Post Office buys one hundred and thirty thousand trees to be made into these poles. Some of these are grown at Windsor and Sandringham, in the Queen's forests, but the large majority come from Scotland. Until a few years ago most of the poles came from Scandinavian countries. That was before Britain benefited by the example of those countries in marking trees in advance, instead of selecting poles from trees which had already been felled.

The men engaged in the selection of these poles must have a

sound knowledge of individual types of tree. They each examine between fifteen and twenty thousand poles a year. Some species of pine, for instance, are so similar to each other that only an expert can distinguish between them. Yet if a mistake were made and one of the more brittle type selected, they might snap and so endanger the lives of the engineers who have to work on them.

In the Telecommunications Exhibition at Fleet House there is an interesting exhibit of a small section of telegraph pole erected in 1895. It has a hole through the centre about eighteen feet from the ground. This was made by woodpeckers! The pole which had previously stood in this position on the same spot had received the same treatment from woodpeckers in the same place. Furthermore, the adjacent pole was damaged in the same manner.

Scots pine, Douglas fir and larch are some of the types of wood best suited for telegraph poles, partly because of their slow growth. It takes between thirty and forty years for a tree to be ready for felling, but with present day power saws it takes only twenty-five seconds to fell the trees.

There are sixteen reasons for rejecting trees and the pole inspector must be completely familiar with these. Inspectors are domiciled in different parts of the country to watch the trees for pests of one kind or another, and to see that the lower branches are lopped off at the appropriate time. They must have a sound knowledge of the different kinds of fungi and insects and their effect. Inspectors keep a watch on the contractors, making sure that the poles are

A woodpecker at work on a telegraph pole

shaped, drilled for standard fittings, and that they are seasoned by remaining in the open for a year before being creosoted. There is also the risk of fire to be guarded against. Once the pole is ready for its task the inspectors stamp their initials on it; in sixteen years of service one inspector has his initials stamped on more than two hundred thousand poles.

Today more poles are taken down than are put in. Between thirty and forty thousand are removed annually. This used to be the task of gangs of at least three men. Now, with only two men and a four-ton lorry equipped with a hydraulic crane, the pole can be jacked out and loaded onto the lorry in fifteen minutes.

Erection, too, has been a heavy task until recently, with the strain and backache of manhandling the poles, as well as digging the holes in which they have to be sunk. Now a special fleet of motor vehicles has been provided, complete with all the mechanical equipment for handling and erecting telegraph poles. Each vehicle can carry nine poles, which is sufficient for a day's work. The lineman still has to climb the pole to fix the wires as each new one is erected. There are also faults to be attended to from time to time, especially after stormy or gusty weather, when obstructions such as branches of trees falling onto the wires can put a whole group of telephones out of order. Heavy snowfalls are another menace to overhead telephone wires, the sheer weight of the snow sometimes bearing the wires down to the ground. It is for these reasons, apart from the unsightliness of overhead wiring, that underground cables are preferred.

Many pairs of wires can be carried in one cable. To peel off the external insulation and protective material and look at the plaited pairs of coloured, insulated wires which run from the telephone to the junction box, and so to the exchange, is to see a very neat piece of work. For the past fifty years the method of joining the wires has been by 'hand twist', a single join taking twenty-five seconds. Recently, a 'jointing' machine has been developed which joins them in three seconds. This gives greater productivity in laying and maintaining cables. There could be as many as three thousand three hundred pairs of wire in each cable, each pair carrying electric current to the point where it is converted into sound waves. The Japanese held the record with four thousand pairs in one cable. Now a British manufacturer has produced one with four thousand eight hundred pairs of wire.

Hundreds of cables from all over the area come into the basement of the exchange, from which they are directed through the main distribution frames to switching gear in the apparatus room above.

Some exchanges have as many as two hundred or more cables

The linesman often has to
repair wires after a
heavy snowfall

coming in. These are fairly rigid and one of the purposes of the distribution frame is to connect these rigid cables to more flexible types. At the same time fuses are put into the circuits to protect the lines from short circuiting or contact with power lines and other accidental faults.

Telephone conversations are private to the subscribers and lines can be tapped legally only on a warrant from a Secretary of State.

Mobile telephone exchanges, wired for immediate use, have been developed to the advantage of areas which have a desperate need for more lines. This means that four hundred lines can be provided quickly, thus helping to reduce the waiting list until permanent lines can be provided, when the exchange can be moved on to other areas.

With the development of electronics, switchboards are gradually being replaced by new cordless switchboards and modern electronic equipment. Operators' headsets have also been improved so that they now weigh less than one ounce, instead of six as formerly, and the headband can be worn round the back of the head.

The history of every line connected to the exchange is recorded on a card, which means that, when any query or fault arises on any subscriber's line, this indexed card can be extracted and provide precise details of everything relating to that particular telephone. Throughout the service, provision is made for constant testing of lines and equipment. In some exchanges engineers are on duty day and night. Many of the faults reported can be diagnosed on the instrument panel over the test desk, thus enabling instructions to be passed on to maintenance engineers without delay.

Since the introduction of electronic exchanges, a machine has been developed to keep a check on the equipment which goes into these exchanges. This machine makes a thousand calls an hour and provides a more thorough test than was possible before its introduction. Known as a 'call sender' it is used in making final tests of equipment as it is assembled at the

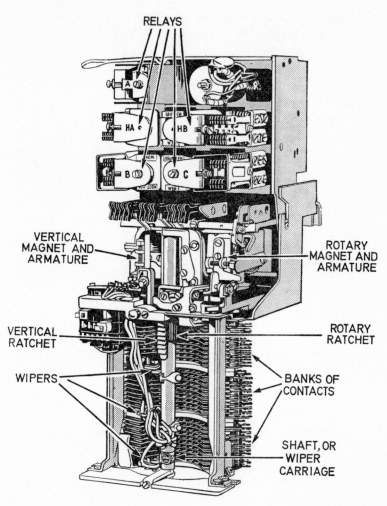

RELAYS

VERTICAL MAGNET AND ARMATURE

ROTARY MAGNET AND ARMATURE

VERTICAL RATCHET

ROTARY RATCHET

WIPERS

BANKS OF CONTACTS

SHAFT, OR WIPER CARRIAGE

Selectors do the work of an operator to a great extent

exchange, as well as diagnosing faults in existing lines. Not only does this tester detect a fault, but also it shows where the fault is and what is causing it. This is a tremendous time saver. Previously a number of engineers were fully employed on this work. Now an operator is 'called' by a fault condition. As an example of the speed of operation, it has been estimated that it would take ten telephonists, working non-stop for eight hours, to do the work that one of these 'call senders' does in an hour. It is hoped, eventually (possibly before this book is published),

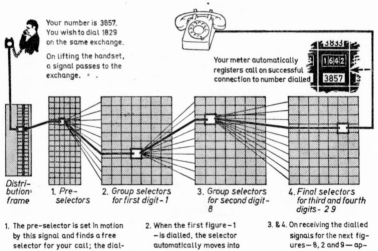

Your number is 3857.
You wish to dial 1829
on the same exchange.

On lifting the handset,
a signal passes to the
exchange.

Your meter automatically
registers call on successful
connection to number dialled

Distri-
bution
frame

1. Pre-
selectors

2. Group selectors
for first digit - 1

3. Group selectors
for second digit -
8

4. Final selectors
for third and fourth
digits - 2 9

1. The pre-selector is set in motion by this signal and finds a free selector for your call; the dialling tone is now heard and the number can be dialled.

2. When the first figure - 1 - is dialled, the selector automatically moves into position to connect the line ready for the next figure.

3. & 4. On receiving the dialled signals for the next figures - 8, 2 and 9 - appropriate selectors move into position automatically to complete the circuit for the number dialled - 1829.

Making a call on a local exchange

that it will be made to work automatically, recording minor faults and operating an alarm signal if it discovers a fault which requires emergency treatment.

The automatic system, whereby calls can be made direct without the necessity to go through the operator at the exchange, has eliminated delays in all services, the subscriber being automatically connected to the required number simply by dialling the necessary digits. In effect, selectors do the work of an operator to a great extent. The selectors in the apparatus room at the exchange each have a hundred contacts, ten in a row. As the first number is dialled the selector automatically steps up to one of the ten levels and moves along to the first disengaged contact. The next number is dealt with by another selector on a different connected set of contacts, and the last two digits by a third selector on yet another set of a hundred contacts. When the last number is dialled the wanted subscriber's telephone rings automatically. The whole operation is performed far more speedily than it could be done by the most efficient operator. In the case of a call which has to be routed through an intermediate exchange, this is done by the use of code numbers which, when dialled, operate switches which select a disengaged junction through which the call can be routed to the required exchange.

Demand trunk dialling was a major development. This simply means that, instead of the subscriber having to wait while the operator routes the call through connecting exchanges, or junctions, connections can be made immediately because the new switchboard gives the operator direct access to all the trunk lines connected to the exchange.

More recently—in December 1958—Subscriber Trunk Dialling (STD) was introduced, making it possible for callers to dial their trunk numbers direct. This was made possible by the introduction of a piece of machinery known as Group Routing and Charging Equipment (GRACE) which, as its name implies, routes and charges the calls as they are made . 'O', when dialled, connects the subscriber to GRACE and the number represents the required town. For example, dialling 'o1' connects the caller through GRACE to London, or 'o21' to Birmingham. By dialling the exchange code and the required subscriber's number, GRACE is instructed to route the call through the network of trunk lines to the exchange and so to the required number. When the caller is connected, GRACE

automatically records the number of chargeable units on the
caller's particular meter, from which the quarterly account is
made up. Thus, subscribers on this system can dial each other
direct regardless of distance. This facility also applies to some
overseas numbers.

Until this system was introduced, a basic charge was made
for trunk calls. This was varied for calls of a greater or lesser
distance. When Subscriber Trunk Dialling was introduced,
charges were revised so that the time and not the basic charge is
varied according to distances.

Last year approximately seven thousand million inland calls
were made, and over eighteen million overseas calls. This
volume of business could not have been handled on a totally
manual basis. By dialling their trunk calls customers have paid
two hundred million pounds less than they would have done
under the manual system for the same number of calls. Yet it is
surprising that about three hundred and sixty million dialled
calls a year are ineffective due to errors made by the customer,
and over seventy million calls were routed unnecessarily through
the operator during 1968-9, while the Directory Enquiries service had sixty million enquiries for numbers which were in local
directories. The elimination of these errors would save the Post
Office six million pounds in any one year.

One of the biggest obstacles to making direct long distance
calls was the fact that the greater the distance the weaker the
signal became. To overcome this, repeaters have been installed
at intervals. By this means the current is amplified as the
circuits pass through the different repeaters until, when it
reaches its destination, its strength has not been impaired.

The invention, in the first place, of the thermionic valve, and
later of transistors, so useful in radio and television, has made
this possible.

For nearly forty years three letters and a set of figures have
been used in big cities when making a telephone call. This
system was adopted with the introduction of automatic telephones in London and was later extended to other big cities.

As the number of subscribers increased to more than six million, with the likelihood of that number being trebled within twenty years, the problem of finding sufficient permutations in sets of three letters which would make a pronounceable word for an exchange was quite considerable. Expectations were that, by 1970, all the three hundred and twenty acceptable combinations for the London area would have been used. On the other hand, by using all-figure dialling, this number is more than doubled. This was only one of the reasons why a change seemed necessary. When subscribers are able to dial their own international calls, a standard dialling system for each country will become essential. Very few other countries have letters on their dials, and with America, Canada and France agreeing to adopt all-figure numbers, it became the sensible thing for Britain to do the same.

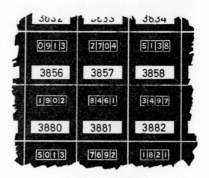

A group of individual subscriber meters

This has involved an enormous amount of work, including sending out information and instructions to telephonists and to the public.

Telephone accounts are now being computerized. Previously they were prepared by clerical assistants with the aid of address plates, ready reckoners and printing and adding machines. Now the meter reading is photographed and translated onto a punched card, while a scanner punches holes in another card showing STD calls made. The customer's name, and details of the account, are then recorded on magnetic tape. In the computer room the account is calculated from the magnetic tape before it is put into the computer's automatic printing machine which produces the bill. Another machine, known as the enveloper, folds each bill, puts it into a window envelope, and seals the envelope before it is posted. This method has more than doubled the number of accounts which can be prepared in a given time.

Revision of telephone directories is another major task, the preparation of which becomes more and more onerous as subscribers increase. As these directories became greater in volume, those covering the London Postal Area were divided into four bulky books, while those covering outer London were issued in seven separate volumes. There are, in all, fifteen directories covering the main areas of England and Scotland, with an additional thirty-eight covering large towns and the areas around them. In addition, for some of the small towns, local directories are issued.

The colossal task of preparing all these telephone directories has normally been done by hand, with special copies kept for alterations and additions. In future, however, this is to be done by computer. Records will be stored in this and amendments fed into it. When a button is pressed the computer will produce a magnetic tape listing all the information in alphabetical order.

Another computer will make any changes required, such as punctuation marks and capital letters. A photo typesetting machine will produce a film of a directory page from the revised magnetic tape. It is anticipated that, by 1972, all directories will be prepared and printed by this method.

Towards the end of 1968 entries in the Manchester local telephone directory were put on microfilm with a view to discovering whether its use would make possible a faster and cheaper Directory Enquiry service. All the three thousand entries in the directory were put on a single transparency the size of a postcard. When an enquiry is made the operator moves the transparency under a viewer to find the required entry. A second method, using a number of transparencies, with a different type of viewer and an index button, was tried out. This would take all seven million directory entries in the United Kingdom. Either of these methods, if successful, would avoid the need for the two thousand directory enquiry operators to keep the full set of sixty-two separate volumes available.

The year 1967 saw the publication of the first of the yellow pages. These were included at the end of the Brighton Area directory, and gave a complete list of all the businesses and trades in the area. When the issue of these becomes nation-wide, in 1970, it is anticipated that the consequent reduction of enquiries which will need to be made will result in a saving to the Post Office of two million pounds a year. It is also expected that, by 1975, this will bring in about twenty-five million pounds a year from advertising revenue, as against the present three million pounds.

In London these classified directories are issued as separate volumes, but elsewhere they are included at the back of the normal directories, though Birmingham, Manchester, Liverpool and Glasgow will also be issued with separate volumes.

In addition to the many business, social and domestic advantages given by the telephone, there are all the special services which it offers.

Perhaps the most important of these is the 999 call for ambulance, fire or police services. When a 999 call is made by a subscriber, or from a call box, a red alarm lamp is lit in the exchange and a buzzer is sounded so that operators at all switchboards are promptly alerted and such calls take precedence over other business. Many a life has been saved, a fire kept within bounds, or a criminal apprehended by means of this service. Numerous instances are recorded of callers failing, for one reason or another, to give the address where the service is required, or even the telephone number of the caller. Yet the operator has been able to trace the call and the service has been provided. One such incident was recorded in West Sussex, when a caller needing urgent medical attention owing to an accident in the home, dialled the operator, said he was bleeding to death, and collapsed before giving his number. The operator kept the call connected while she contacted a lineman, who was able to trace the call and arrange for emergency services to go into action. When the caller was admitted to hospital it was found that he had lost six pints of blood. The man owed his life to the quick-thinking operator who had kept the line open and to the lineman who had traced the call.

The recorded message device is another of the special services which is being increasingly installed in subscribers' premises. This enables messages or orders to be given by telephone after the office has closed, or when the individual subscriber is out. It is also used by some libraries for renewal of books. By dialling a stated number it is possible to obtain a weather or road report, be given the cricket score, or even a cookery recipe. TIM, the speaking clock, whose all-figure number is 123, is the oldest and most used of the special telephone services. More than six calls a second were made on this circuit during 1966–7. TIM alone, of the special services, is completely automatic. For the other services forty telephonists are trained to make the recordings as the information comes in. A report giving the weather news comes through from the meteorological office once an hour. During Test Matches, if a team is scoring quickly, the wire is rarely silent. One telephonist takes down the score, another makes the recording and the third checks it before it is put out to the public. For the 'dial-a-disc' service for Leeds and Newcastle, a different pop-song is recorded every night. With eighty thousand calls a week for this in the north of England, the service is likely to be extended to many other centres.

The operators recording these different services speak into microphones and the recordings are made automatically on magnetic discs in the engineering studio where TIM is housed.

These information services have become so successful that many ideas have been put forward for more such services in the future. These include 'Dial-a-Prayer', 'Dial Santa Claus', 'Dial the Football Results'.

The car radiophone is another service which has become popular. A politician, business man, representative or other person can have a radiophone installed in his car for a comparatively small fee, but calls are charged at a higher rate than those made from a normal house or business telephone. In the case of the London Radiophone service, a subscriber can make a call from any part of the seven hundred square miles of Greater London.

Subscribers buy or rent a set from a manufacturer approved by the Post Office and the manufacturer will maintain it. Installation is very simple. A small box of equipment is placed in the boot of the car. The control panel in the front of the car contains several switches. When the set is switched on, a calling lamp is operated. In London each service area has three connecting channels to each of the North-Eastern, North-Western and Southern areas. These are clearly shown on a map which is provided with each set. Red, yellow and blue buttons are pressed to connect with the different areas. In addition to these nine channels there is a Control Channel by means of which the exchange can signify that it wishes to connect a call to the car. The subscriber can also use this to contact the exchange if he is in difficulty. In the event of a channel being engaged when a subscriber switches to it, a Channel Engaged lamp will light and the subscriber can try another channel.

The radiophone is simple to use when travelling in the service area. First the set must be switched to the Control Channel. The switch must remain on all the time the car is in use in order that calls in and out may be connected. The set must also be switched to the connecting channel serving the particular area in which the car is stationary. Calls can be made while a car is in motion but, for road safety reasons, subscribers are urged to stop when making or receiving a call.

When the operator connects a call to a subscriber's radiophone, besides being able to observe the glow of the calling lamp, the subscriber who is called will hear a discreet buzzer. When answering, the subscriber must lift his instrument, operate the call button and give his number in the normal manner. He will then be asked to switch to the requisite channel. The 'press to talk' switch must be operated when speaking, and released when listening. In the event of an incoming call being made when the car is unattended, the operator will hold the call and try later.

Subscribers have individual radiophone numbers which are printed in the telephone directory immediately under their ordinary numbers.

Just over two years ago one large business concern had a special telephone installation put in its new office at a cost of one and a half million pounds! Needless to say, this has many modern refinements which are supplied only on special request. These include a very big electronic exchange, nine thousand push-button telephones, a separate internal network, facilities for incoming calls to be dialled direct to extensions, fifty private wires to branches throughout the country, as well as a computer linked to the exchange! This computer not only does most of the dialling by storing nearly three thousand of the numbers most frequently used by this business, but also will not pass unauthorized calls. In addition, it gives different facilities for different phones. Most of the staff have a telephone linked to the computer for outside calls, and a second instrument for internal calls, both of which have push-buttons instead of dials.

Many of the internal phones are linked to dictating machines so that letters dictated into the phone are recorded on a disc which is collected by the typist. These have the same advantages as an ordinary dictaphone, having buttons on the top of the instrument which give facilities for start, stop and playback.

The system was designed, built and installed by a telecommunications contractor, the Post Office being responsible for fitting it into the national network, testing and maintaining it.

The ever increasing use of the telephone and the continuing demand for more and more installations is sufficient evidence that the telephone is fulfilling a very necessary service to the community.

10

Cables and Cable Ships

Although cables are much less liable to damage than overhead wires, a workman's drill can easily put them out of action. One such case occurred near Faraday House, where the International Telephone Exchange is situated.

Technicians were quickly on the spot and engineers made the usual tests to locate the trouble before opening up the cable to reveal a thousand pairs of wires. Each pair had to be tested and, where necessary, jointed together again. In this kind of work only a limited number of men can be employed at a time. For two days and nights they worked, four men to a shift, to make temporary repairs which would enable the circuits to operate. Later, a new length of cable had to be laid.

Floods are another threat to cables, though efforts are constantly being made to make them impervious to bad weather conditions. In the disastrous floods in the West Country in 1968, bridges were washed away carrying telephone cables with them. Nearly thirty-nine thousand telephone lines were cut, causing damage to Post Office equipment and installations to the value of nearly half a million pounds.

Engineers worked without a break—some for as long as thirty-six hours at a time—making temporary repairs to get the telephone service, so urgently needed, operating again. In twelve days all was patched up and working, though the engineers, who followed later to do the permanent restoration, had many months of hard work before the job was completed. In one area there were so many faults that more phones were put out of action in one night than normally happens in a year. With the equally disastrous floods which occurred throughout most of the country later in the same year, still more damage was caused to telephone equipment.

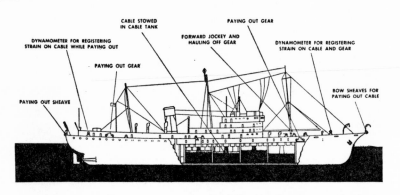

The cable laying ship *Monarch* can operate in any depth of water

Over four million miles of cable is required by the Post Office each year. Much of this is needed by the Submarine Branch. This is the department which deals with those cables going under water and it controls the four cable ships which lay them.

The *Monarch* was the first British Post Office cable ship. The present ship is the fourth *Monarch*. The first, a wooden paddle vessel fitted as a cable ship, was condemned in 1870. The second, but the first to be built as a cable ship in 1883, was sunk by a mine during the 1914–18 war. The third, built in 1916, had a similar fate, this time in the Second World War, being sunk in 1945. For some time the fourth and present *Monarch* was the biggest cable ship in the world, but she went into second place when a German ship of twelve thousand tons was built, as against *Monarch*'s eight thousand four hundred and thirty-two tons. *Monarch*'s speed is twelve knots and she can operate in any depth. In her four tanks she can carry nearly six thousand tons or one thousand two hundred and thirty miles of cable.

The Post Office has four of these ships. The *Monarch* is based at Greenwich and is constantly laying new cables. Among other important tasks she laid cables in the Commonwealth Pacific Cables system (known as COMPAC), which provides a trans-atlantic telephone service between this country and Canada and across the Pacific Ocean to join Canada with Australia and New Zealand, via Hawaii and Fiji. The Pacific Ocean cable, completed by the end of 1963, was then the biggest single tele-communications project ever undertaken and the longest sub-marine cable which had been laid. When the Queen made the inaugural call on this system her voice travelled sixteen thousand miles, and was clearly heard simultaneously in the five countries linked by these cables. Besides increasing the speech channels, COMPAC opened up twenty-two teleprinter channels, enabled circuits to be leased to airlines, shipping companies and other commercial enterprises, and provided facilities for the transmission of music, pictures and broad-casting.

The *Alert* is the most recent ship and is based at Glasgow. She is mostly engaged in North Atlantic protection controls, going off to Grand Banks in Newfoundland to protect the cables from damage by ice or by trawlers. This area is criss-crossed with cables. It is also a very good fishing ground for ships from all over the world. Not only do trawlers' nets and otter boards do considerable damage, but expensive fishing gear is lost by entanglement with the cables.

The *Iris* and the *Ariel*, based at Woolwich and Dover respectively, are out at sea most of the time doing repair work, or dropping and recovering guiding buoys before and after cable laying.

When a new cable has to be laid the Company which makes it charters the ship. The commander, pursers, navigating officers and crew are Post Office staff, but the cable company sends its own representatives, as well as its own jointers.

About a year before the cable has to be laid, a ship is sent to make a complete survey of the ocean bottom, after which a profile and charts are drawn up in order that the best route can be worked out. This means that those responsible for laying it know exactly where the cable is to go, how much is required, and where repeaters are to be inserted.

These repeaters, which are amplifiers contained in waterproof steel cylinders, costing about thirty thousand pounds each, have to be joined into the cable while it is being laid. As their name suggests, repeaters renew the transmission power over the long distance cables. They can be jointed into the cable while the ship is still moving. All the cable required is coiled neatly down below in the four tanks, but the repeaters are left on deck. The number of those which can be accommodated on deck controls the amount of cable laying which can be done on one trip.

These repeaters are made in something like a hospital, or dust-free surgery; the men who work there wear masks. This is because the repeaters have moving parts and it is important that no particle of dust shall interfere with their working. Five sheave gears go over and under each repeater to keep the right tension, and each repeater has two parachutes clipped on the outside.

Some cables are laid well below the sea bed, one laid between Harwich and Landguard Point, near Felixstowe, being eighteen feet below in parts. This is because the cable, which carries trunk traffic from Ipswich to London, was frequently being damaged by ships anchoring in Harwich docks. Sinking it to a depth of eighteen feet below the sea bed avoids the risk of damage when a deep water channel for big ships is being dredged.

To make it safe from trawlers it is necessary to bury it only about six feet, though burying cable is a costly business anyway. These cables have a capacity of one thousand one hundred and forty telephone circuits, which is more than twice as much as any other system. It could be very costly if these were damaged by trawlers.

To bury this cable a sea plough is used. This has a hollow blade through which the cable is run. It is rammed into the sea bed and the ship drags it along, the cable running out through the hollow. Nozzles in the front of the blade direct high pressure water jets into the sea bed, thrusting the silt aside.

Before the ship starts on one of these trips, the end of the cable is fixed to the shore repeater station and so through a little hut back from the beach and out to the ship. It is more usual for cable to be put over the stern of the ship and the vessel controlled from aft. The ship does four to five knots when laying cable but reduces speed while repeaters are put in.

Submarine cable of the older type will twist when under tension while being paid out. In 1952 the Post Office Research Station at Dollis Hill started to design a completely new type of coaxial cable for use in deep water. This is lightweight, the most important feature being that it will not twist when under tension. Several thousands of turns are made in it when it is stored in the ship.

After the first seven miles the cable is cut and the first repeater jointed in. Two instruments, known as dynamometers, one on either side of the ship, measure the tension of the cable in hundredweights, while another instrument shows the speed at which it is being paid out.

On the bridge is a Decca instrument which compares radio signals. This is used to find the position of the ship. It is most important that other ships shall not come in the path of the cable as it is being laid. Officers of the watch have no time to keep a constant look-out for other vessels, but there are three special lights which take care of this. They are red, white and red, set vertically, to warn other craft that cable is being laid.

All cables have a mile mark which assists the plotting. Someone calls through a microphone which mile mark is going out. Everyone on the ship can hear this, from the control room where the operator stands, to the bridge where the cable officer stands. Accuracy is most important and the cable is being tested in the test room all the time to ensure that nothing is going wrong while it is being laid. Signals are sent along the cable to the shore station to test whether everything is going as it should. If anything is wrong the ship must be stopped. This can and does happen.

The tanks in which the cable is stored are filled with water to prevent it becoming overheated by its own weight and bursting into flames. These tanks are fifteen to twenty feet deep, therefore a lot of weight is pressing down on to the bottom layer.

The chief engineer decides how fast the engines must go and how fast the cable shall be paid out. He adjusts the speed and says how much percentage slack should be used. A wire which leads to the sea bed and back to the ship indicates how far the ship has travelled.

In the deck department are the captain, the navigating officers, cable officers and seamen, while in the engine room department are the engineering officers, the stackers and the greasers. Three pursers deal with wireless, customs and immigration and attend to the testing equipment. When going into port, immigration officers have to be seen and customs duty paid on cable brought into the country. On the technical staff are testing officers and jointers who are concerned solely with the cable. The catering department provides meals for the whole ship.

Before ships go out to repair cables which are damaged, shore engineers send a pulse along the cable. This stops at the point of the fault, and measurements can then be taken to discover how far the pulse has travelled.

The ship is sent out provided with this information which enables the engineers to find the fault from the known position of where the cable is laid. When this is found, a rope with a four- or five-pronged hook on the end is put down and dragged along the bottom of the ocean until the cable is hooked. This is a fairly simple operation when it is lying on the sea bed, though, because of strong currents, it takes about eight hours to put the

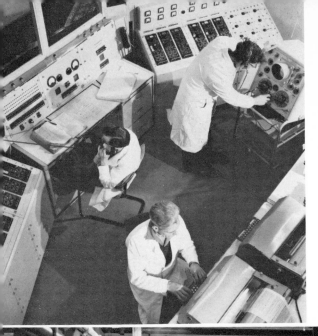

Working in the Central Control position at Rugby Radio Station and, *below*, a general view showing Concentric Feeder Lines and Aerial Changeover Switchboards, together with an STC Transmitter being tuned

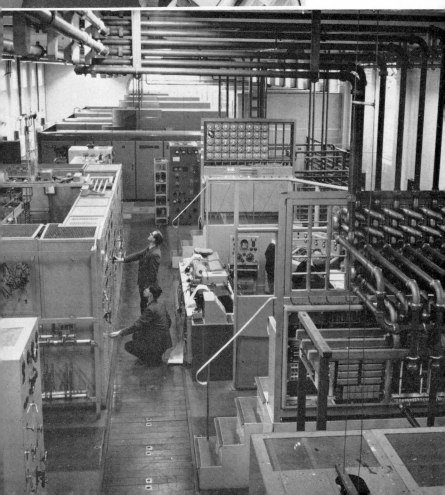

A Television Detector car showing the panoramic receiver and, *below*, an operator is tuning the aerial handwheel of the panoramic receiver

A microwave aerial at Ballygomartin Radio Station

The bowl of the aerial at Goonhilly Downs Radio Station is
ninety feet across

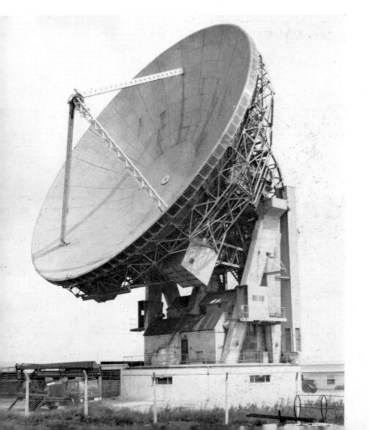

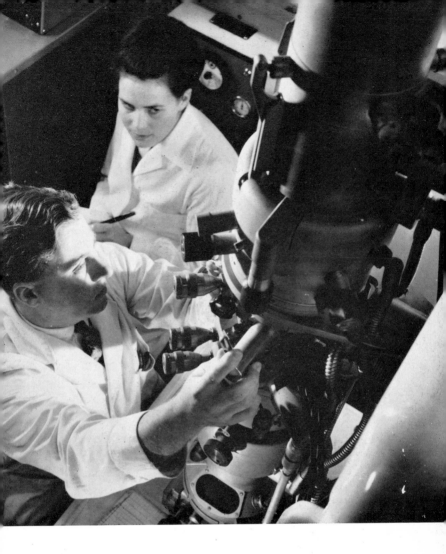

(*Top left*) The Goonhilly aerial can be steered automatically by the control console to point to any part of the sky

(*Left*) The main control building is in the centre of the site at Goonhilly Downs

(*Above*) Inserting a specimen into an electron microscope at Dollis Hill Research Station

Technicians under instruction at a telecommunications training school

Telephonists undergoing a Directory Enquiry training trial

The conference table in a Confravision studio. The business meeting is linked by sound and vision to another studio in a different part of the country

hook down and find the cable. If it is buried, the prong has to dig into the sand until the weight of the cable is shown on the dynamometer. The ship is then stopped, the cable hooked up onto the deck, and repair work can begin. After repair the cable is returned to the sea bed in the same manner.

All this is comparatively straightforward, but it is not as simple when icy or stormy conditions are encountered. For several months each year cable ships from this country work with French and Canadian ships from a base at St John's, Newfoundland. Their job is to keep open transatlantic telephone lines by warning the fishing fleet to stay clear of cables laid on the sea bed. Carrying warning signs in many languages, and with repair equipment, the ships patrol an area where the temperature often drops to thirty-six degrees below freezing point. Frequently the ships become encrusted with ice which may be eighteen inches thick.

Little is heard about Post Office sailors who work under arctic conditions to keep open these lines of communication, or of those who are subjected to hazardous weather conditions when laying new cables.

A typical example of this is the story of the *Alert* when she steamed out of Southampton in September 1964, with a hundred miles of cable and eight repeaters on board, to be laid between Britain and Holland. It was a pleasant summery day, and the conditions seemed ideal. If this weather had continued the job could have been completed within twenty-four hours. In the event it took nine full days.

The ship set out to drop a guiding buoy a third of the way along the route, before going to pick up the shore end of the cable which had been laid some months previously, about twenty-five miles out from the Suffolk coast. This was soon found and lifted from the sea bed, but as the six-hour task of joining the two ends was about to begin, such a strong wind blew up that it became impossible to keep the ship steady. The only way was to fix a buoy on the shore end of the cable and let it go into the sea again until the weather improved. All night the ship waited. The next morning a message was received that the electrician's mother had died suddenly. The captain ordered the ship back to the coast, while arrangements were made for the bereaved man to be taken off in a fishing vessel so that he could travel on to his home in Glasgow. The ship lay at anchor all that day, waiting for the necessary twenty-four-hour forecast of favourable weather conditions. It was four days after the ship had left Southampton before conditions were sufficiently favourable for the cable to be picked up again.

On the afternoon of the fourth day the two ends were joined and the ship went on its way, laying the cable throughout the night.

About thirty miles of cable and two repeaters had been laid when, the next morning, the wind suddenly blew up again. The captain gave the order for the ship to stop and, while the helmsman fought to hold the vessel steady, anxious eyes watched the dial on the dynamometer record the tension on the cable while the wind increased in violence. Then the captain gave the order to cut the cable, an order which is never given except under direst necessity.

The cable, which had already been picked up twice, was cut and slid back into the sea. Another six hours' work would be needed to join it again when weather conditions allowed.

Throughout the day the storm raged and the ship lay at anchor. The next day the wind abated sufficiently for the discarded end to be picked up, jointed, and cable laying to continue. A third repeater went over the side and laying went on for another two hours before the storm broke again. On this occasion it was decided not to release the cable, though at one time the dials recording the tension showed that the point of strain was only three tons below danger level.

The ship was due for its annual refit and consequently had on board only sufficient supplies for a normal run. Cigarettes and drinks began to get low. The Amsterdam berth had been booked only until the Tuesday, and this was already Saturday. They had three days more. The ship had been at sea a week, with only three of the eight repeaters laid. For a day and a half the vessel rode at anchor, holding the cable. On the evening of the second day laying was resumed, but only for two hours, with one more repeater laid. Once more the ship lay at anchor with a force eight gale blowing.

The captain studied the weather forecasts. With a huge depression building up over the west coast of England it was obvious the weather would worsen the next day. They must go on laying the cable through the night in spite of navigational problems.

Early next morning, with due ceremony, the last repeater was despatched. All that night they worked, and throughout the next day they were clearing up and stowing away. At five o'clock in the afternoon they docked at Amsterdam, their job at last completed on the final day that the berth had been reserved.

CHAPTER

11

International Telephone Service

Two hundred calls an hour to America every afternoon is a fair average estimate of the volume of business with that country. When such calls were first made they cost fifteen pounds for three minutes, but now that the service is so popular the charge is much less.

These, and calls of considerably greater distance, go out from the International Telephone Exchange at Faraday Building, Queen Victoria Street, London E.C.4, which has for many years been the hub of the main trunk routes in this country and overseas. This was one of the first long-distance exchanges in the world. Today, in ten acres of floor space, there are five completely automatic exchanges, seven auto-manual exchanges, and six hundred and seventy-five operating positions. Although seven million calls are made through automatic equipment every week, operators handle as many as fifty thousand inland long-distance, approximately seventy thousand European, and sixteen thousand international calls. Most operators at this international exchange speak two or three languages, for which they receive an additional salary.

Because signals decrease in strength with the distance travelled, it was necessary to find means of amplifying and boosting the signals as they travelled. This has been solved by the introduction of valves—there are sixty thousand of them and their associated equipment at Faraday House—and repeaters such as those used in cables. Signals may be amplified by as much as a million times their original strength. This, combined with the use which can be made of radio microwaves, has made it possible today to speak to almost any country in the world. For instance, in the case of a call to Australia, the Atlantic cable takes the call as far as Montreal, where it is picked up by microwave to Vancouver. There the Commonwealth cable takes it on the remainder of its journey via Fiji, Auckland, New Zealand and so to the Australian subscriber required. It would appear from this that the connection of a call over such a distance would take a considerable time. In actual fact it takes less time than it does to explain how it works. Such a call, covering a distance of sixteen thousand miles, can be made in three seconds flat. One of the more recent pieces of equipment which have helped to reduce the time of connecting such calls at the exchange is 'key-sending'. This is a comparatively new form of dialling, which is performed by depressing a limited number of keys in a small unit, thereby obtaining the full benefit of the speed of electronic equipment.

Many international calls are transmitted from one of the Post Office radio stations, such as the one at Rugby where the tallest masts are eight hundred and twenty feet high. At this station, in January 1927, the first long-distance radio telephone service to America was opened.

Perhaps the most valuable use of the radio telephone service is that which keeps ships in touch with each other and with land through coast radio stations. To enable this to be done effectively the various shipping companies send to Faraday House a monthly chart of sailings. Ten thousand ships in every part of the world can now be reached by radio telephone. Only the larger vessels have qualified medical staff on board, but if a seaman is taken ill while at sea, medical advice can be obtained from the radio operator at the coast station by means of the radio

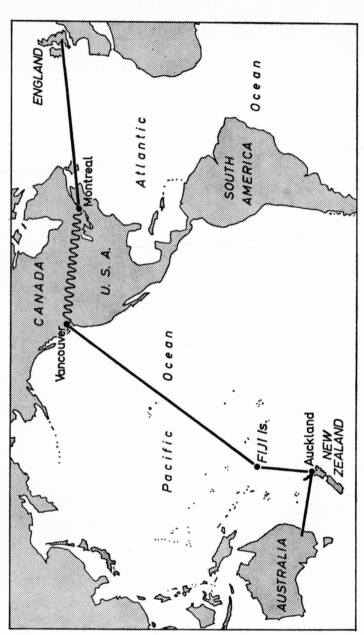

A telephone call is carried by cable and microwave to Australia

telephone. All nations' ships around Britain's coasts can have the benefit of this service and as many as three hundred and fifty medical cases are dealt with in one year by this means.

Weather bulletins are broadcast and there is also a direction-finding service which enables ships to fix their position. Shipping and fishing concerns can make radio telephone calls to their skippers advising them of the best fishing grounds, or asking a ship to make a call to pick up additional cargo, resulting in saving of money and time. The service is also useful to the crew, enabling them to keep in touch with their families ashore.

Radio coast stations keep a constant watch for distress calls. When these are received the whole station gets busy alerting ships and keeping in touch with rescue operations.

By ringing the International Telephone Exchange at Faraday House, anyone wishing to make a radio telephone call to a ship can be connected, even if the ship is on the other side of the world. The charge for this service is dependent on distance, the minimum charge being twelve shillings and sixpence.

A more up-to-date international telephone centre has now been built in London to supplement the Faraday international exchange, as well as to provide additional capacity for handling the increasing volume of traffic. This new centre is the most advanced of its kind and has extended international subscriber dialling (ISD), putting STD subscribers here in direct dialling contact with many more countries than was possible before. The international maintenance centre has the most advanced fault-finding equipment in the world, by means of which an engineer can test each circuit merely by sitting at a control console and touching a button. The two computers at the centre keep a constant watch on its running and calculate each nation's share of international telephone accounts.

Yet another, and still bigger, international exchange is to be built on a site next to Cannon Street Station. This is to cope with further growth in this immense business of telecommunications. Obviously there is nothing static about telecommunications; the Post Office must constantly be planning for the future.

12

The Tallest Building in England

Year by year the public become more and more telephone conscious, resulting in an ever-increasing pressure on existing facilities. For years the demand has been far greater than the supply of telephones, or the available lines. Trunk calls have shown an increase of 17 per cent a year, which suggests that this traffic alone could double in a few years. Overseas traffic is also likely to be doubled. At present there is a telephone in one home in four. By 1973 two homes in five will have one.

In addition to the increasing use of the telephone, the Post Office was faced with the task of arranging for an increasing number of channels for television, especially those required for the extension of B.B.C.2 and colour television.

The problem of providing adequate facilities for this volume of traffic in telecommunications has, for many years, been a matter of urgent consideration. Yet an alternative to the expense and disruption of cable laying, especially in the busy streets of large towns, was needed.

The use of microwaves was the answer. Microwave radio uses wavelengths much shorter than those used for radio or television broadcasting; in fact, the frequencies are so high that the radio begins to behave like light, and can be focussed into narrow pencil beams by aerials shaped like the reflector of a car's headlights. These narrow beams can be used to carry either television or telephony signals from one point to another.

This use of a microwave system gives facilities for carrying as many as eighteen hundred telephone calls on one carrier wave. Alternatively, a single carrier can take either eighteen hundred telephone channels or a television picture, while a

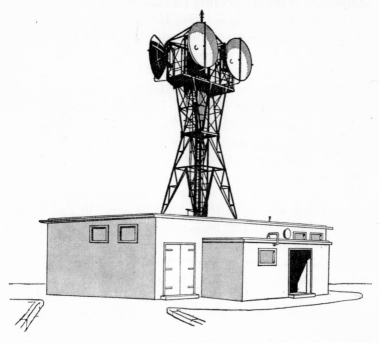

The microwave aerials are shaped like the reflectors of a car's headlights

complete microwave route, fully equipped with many aerials, repeaters, etc., could carry fifty thousand calls, or forty television programmes. The British Post Office is now one of the world's major microwave users, and operates one of the most densely-packed systems in the world.

Two major problems had to be solved before microwaves could be used in this way. The first was that they travel only in a straight line and will not pass through obstacles such as hills or tall buildings; and secondly that they lose power after a distance of thirty miles.

The obvious answer was to build a tower in the centre of London, such a tower to be higher than any other building. To combat the problem of distance, a chain of towers must be built at intervals of twenty to thirty miles to act as repeater stations. When the whole project is completed there will be ninety such towers set at strategic points throughout the country, which will act as repeaters for the telephone and television traffic.

Having decided this, the next problem for those entrusted with the task was to select a place for the London tower to be built. The site of the Museum Exchange offered the best possibilities since there was sufficient ground belonging to the Post Office adjacent to the Exchange, and there was already a network of cables and television links coming into the building.

The clearing of the site for the five hundred and eighty foot tower, which was to be the highest building in Britain, was begun in July 1961. This tower was to be the base for a micro-wave telecommunication system which was to link the whole country through other towers in the large industrial cities. The London tower took five years to build and cost nine million pounds.

A great many points had to be considered when designing the tower, perhaps the most important being its strength and wind resistance. Tall structures, such as the tower envisaged, bend when subjected to high wind pressure. Because microwaves travel so exactly in straight lines, the slightest deviation of the dish and horn aerials to be set near the top of the building could make the whole thing valueless from this point of view.

A reinforced, two feet thick concrete wall was built round the site. To overcome the problem of wind resistance, a hollow, reinforced concrete central shaft was built, the different floors cantilevering out to the external walls of the tower, many with anti-sun-glass windows to prevent overheating. The lower part of the shaft is thirty-five feet in diameter, the walls of it being

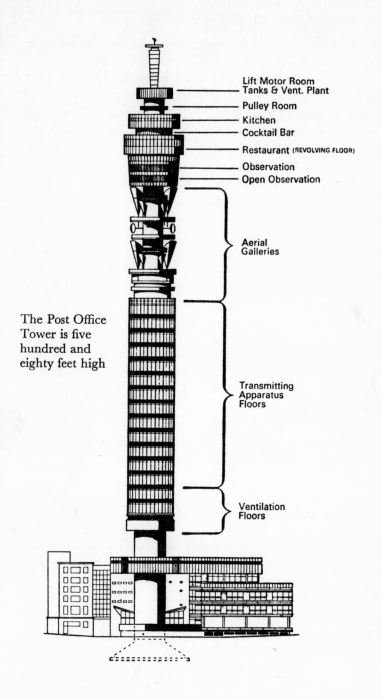

Lift Motor Room
Tanks & Vent. Plant
Pulley Room
Kitchen
Cocktail Bar
Restaurant (REVOLVING FLOOR)
Observation
Open Observation

Aerial
Galleries

The Post Office
Tower is five
hundred and
eighty feet high

Transmitting
Apparatus
Floors

Ventilation
Floors

two feet thick. The upper part of the shaft is reduced in diameter and the walls are less than two feet thick.

Eighty feet above ground level the shaft is linked to the main building by a thick concrete collar which gives additional stability to the tower. In spite of all this protection from wind velocity, when the wind force is greater than twenty knots, the speed of each of the two lifts housed in the shaft is reduced to six hundred feet per minute. Normally these lifts travel up to the top of the tower at a rate of one thousand feet per minute. The shaft also houses an emergency staircase, as well as electricity and telecommunication cables, ventilation ducts and water and sanitary pipes.

The actual building of such a shaft presented unusual problems. A climbing-type crane was used and this rose sixteen feet a day as the shaft was constructed, until eventually it was six hundred feet up. When the crane driver wished to communicate with his colleagues below he had to use a radio telephone.

In the Museum Exchange building, which is associated with the tower, are two large trunk switching units, one to handle STD traffic going out of London and the other, known as 'Mercury', to deal with trunk traffic coming into London.

The five lower floors of the tower house the ventilation and refrigeration plant, as well as batteries and power units. Above those are the apparatus floors with switching and radio equipment.

The British Broadcasting Corporation rent transmission facilities from the Post Office for the whole country, dealing with switching for such things as local news and regional programmes. The task of the Post Office is simply that of ensuring the quality and continuity of the service, and for this purpose a constant watch is kept on the television monitors.

In the case of the Independent Television Authority, the situation is more complex. All the switchings—and there are as many as five thousand a month—are done at the Post Office Tower. One hundred and fifty circuits may have to be altered in a day. There are forty outgoing circuits and any of them can be connected to thirty incoming circuits. Five days in advance of the programme, the Network Switching Unit at the tower receives a schedule from ITA. On the day prior to production of the programme, amendments come in from the contractors, with a few arriving on the actual day. Expensive electronic equipment is installed in order that programmes can be switched speedily and accurately according to the schedule supplied.

The aerial galleries in the tower are situated above the apparatus floors. These galleries are the vital part of the whole microwave system, though they occupy little more than a hundred feet. They contain horn and dish aerials, shaped as their names suggest. Situated all round the galleries, they act as mirrors, transmitting and receiving radio beams to and from the repeater towers set in many different directions.

Above the aerial galleries are three observation platforms enclosed by two bands of double glazed windows. These provide an exciting panoramic view of London for the thousands of visitors who queue for admission daily. Still higher are the cocktail lounge and restaurant, its revolving floor giving diners an ever-changing view of London.

At the top of the tower are the kitchens, to which supplies of food for the restaurant have to be transported daily from the ground floor before the lifts are required for other uses. The forty-foot lattice mast on the roof has a storm warning radar scanner, which is connected to the meteorological office in Holborn. This brings the full height of tower and mast to six hundred and twenty feet.

A high standard of reliability is essential to the maintenance of the service for which the tower has been built. To ensure this, testing goes on all through the day. In addition, stand-by channels have been provided which automatically come into use should a breakdown in the normal channels occur.

One of the radio paths from the tower goes out to the satellite communication ground station at Goonhilly Downs in Cornwall.

13

Space Age Communications

A high piece of flat ground, a mile square, where snow and ice are practically unknown, and wind speeds not particularly bad; that is the site on which the earth station in this country was built.

Situated in the extreme south of Cornwall, Goonhilly Downs was sufficiently solitary to be clear of interference from other radio stations. With a thousand feet of rock in the area the engineers knew where to drive in the piles on which the huge aerial was to be based.

It was July 1961 when the Post Office took over the site, the nearest neighbour being a naval helicopter airfield. Within a year the earth station, with its roads, buildings, aerial control centre and immense amount of complex equipment, was ready and working, making this country the first to engage in telephony tests, the first to transmit live television pictures from Europe by satellite, and the first to transmit colour television. Britain has maintained her position in this field of operation, with no country being able to build a better earth station. No one, in fact, is ahead of us in this business. Delegates from every country in the world have been to Goonhilly to gather information in order to build similar stations in their own country.

The **giant** steerable aerials are the most obvious features of this station. The main control building is in the centre of the site. This houses all the special equipment for the conversion of television pictures and telephone calls into radio frequencies which travel through space. In fact, this building is an operational control centre, a laboratory, a computer centre, a repeater station and a telegraph office in one.

The station, as operated in 1962, cost three-quarters of a million pounds to build and the type of aerial built then was the same as that used at present. The design chosen was originated by Dr Husband, who built the Jodrell Bank aerial. It is a dish type aerial, weighing over a thousand tons, the bowl being eighty-five feet across, with the centre one inch thick and painted grey. The second aerial, built in 1968, is basically the same but the bowl is ninety feet across. When this began to operate, the first aerial was given a million pound refit, most of the money being spent on new transmitters and equipment to handle the increasing number of telephone channels. The twenty-four steel petals which make up the bowl were each made separately, then put in position, and the bowl pivoted so that it can be moved in any direction. The aerial structure is such that if a helicopter were to drop on it, more damage would be done to the helicopter than to the aerial.

When the work was completed it was given what is known as a 'soak test'; it was switched on and left alone for a fortnight.

The sixty-one earth stations are the responsibility of the country in which they are sited, but the actual operation of satellites is managed by the Communications Satellite Corporation of the United States (COMSAT), under agreement with the countries which contribute to the organization. America, as the biggest user, contributes 53 per cent of the working capital, with Great Britain, as the second largest user, giving only 7 per cent, while Germany and France contribute 5 per cent.

Through the Post Office, Great Britain is a shareholder of the International Telecommunications Satellite Corporation (Intelsat), whose fifteen-nation committee made the decision in

Washington, early in 1966, to go ahead with a global commercial communications satellite system. Early experiments
had been made with balloons one hundred miles above the
earth, those known as Echo 1
and Echo 2 being examples.
Echo 2 can still be seen from
Britain when conditions are
favourable.

Telstar was the first satellite put into orbit. Used in
the experimental stage, it was
a medium altitude satellite
which travelled around the
earth making eight orbits a
day, and was able to be used
only when it was over the
Atlantic, and visible from
both stations.

Telstar was the first satellite put
into orbit

The next satellite to be used for communications was known
as Relay, while Early Bird, the satellite launched in April 1965,
was still in use when Intelsat III was launched, at the end of
1968. This was precisely positioned and brought into commercial service early in 1969, and now serves the Atlantic
region, replacing Early Bird. This satellite has more than
four times the capacity of Early Bird, and is being used to
transmit telephony and television between Europe and the
Americas. It is stationed at an altitude of twenty-three thousand
miles over the equator, moving in synchronization with
the rotation of the earth, and therefore appearing to be
almost stationary, making its use possible for twenty-four
hours a day.

Once a communications satellite is successfully launched it
stays in orbit, and consequently there are seven hundred and
seventy satellites of various kinds moving around in space.
These are commonly termed space junk. America has been
responsible for five hundred and fourteen of these, Russia for

two hundred and fifty-three, and our own country for only three.

At present there are sixteen earth terminal stations in twelve different countries and more are under construction. China and Nigeria will be the next, during 1969, followed by Sweden, the Arab Republic and Turkey.

Another satellite, was positioned over the Indian Ocean in the summer of 1969. This has brought a newly equipped Goonhilly aerial into direct communication with the eastern hemisphere, thus completing a satellite link all round the world.

There is one very real problem. While two-way telephone conversations are possible, there is a time lag of about three-fifths of a second for the voice to travel the forty-five thousand mile round trip into space. This is a greater drawback than would appear at first sight. This fact must be recognized by both caller and called, and each be prepared to wait for just over a second for the speech to reach their opposite number and the response to come back before continuing the conversation. Otherwise, they could both be talking at once, yet each hearing what had been said three-fifths of a second earlier, each person becoming more and more impatient because the conversation did not appear to make sense.

The satellite is, basically, a small radio station. Early Bird was fifty to sixty inches in diameter, weighing two hundred pounds, getting its power from the sun. Besides the radio apparatus, the satellite contains two little engines which move it in space. The later satellites, which are very much larger, are multi-access. This makes it possible for a large number of earth stations to transmit and receive from them at the same time.

In the case of telephone calls or television programmes between Britain and America, the satellite receives the speech through the medium of radio microwave signals transmitted through the aerial from the earth station at Goonhilly. These signals are amplified and transmitted to he tdistant ground station aerial in America. Incoming television signals go through Goonhilly to the Post Office Tower where the switching position governs the whole of the country. At Goonhilly a man sits at a console to check the quality of the picture on the four monitoring screens. One shows what is going out, another what is going into the transmitter; the third what is leaving the aerial and the fourth the picture which comes in through the satellite.

The Goonhilly aerial can be steered automatically to point to any part of the sky, following the course of the satellite even when it is subject to wind pressures of seventy miles an hour. Signals transmitted from the satellite giving its position are fed into a computer, which controls the setting of the aerial, enabling it to follow the satellite to an accuracy of one-fifteenth of a degree. In effect, the satellite tells the aerial where to move. As the apparent position of the satellite varies from time to time, the whole aerial will move by up to two degrees in any direction.

When the aerial sends signals to the satellite, high transmitting powers can be used and directed from the aerial onto the satellite, thus creating no problems regarding the distance to be travelled, or the reception of weak signals.

Because the transmitter on the satellite is limited to one or two watts, and the signals sent out are dispersed over a wide area, the aerial picks up a minute amount of power. It is like switching on a radio two hundred and forty thousand miles away on the moon, then sitting back at home trying to hear it. It is no more than a ten billionth part of the power emitted from an ordinary one-watt torch bulb. In other words, if the power from a torch bulb is divided by ten, and the result is divided by a million, and the result of that by another million, that is the amount of power which is being received from the satellite.

This could create quite a problem, especially as the signals received must be separated from radio noise. To deal with the amplification of this a tiny steel cabin has been fixed to the back of the steel bowl. In the cabin is a super-sensitive receiver called a maser, which amplifies these minute radio signals without impairing their quality. The name 'maser' is derived from the initial letters of the words describing what it does, namely, **m**icrowave **a**mplification by the **s**timulated **e**mission of **r**adiation.

The working life of a satellite is about five years, but a new generation of global satellites, known as Intelsat IV, is being designed by international planners. These will be nearly four times as heavy as the present ones and will each be able to handle six thousand two-way telephone conversations. Three of these large capacity satellites over the main ocean regions could provide a space communication system to meet world needs until the 1980's.

As far as possible, earth stations are so constructed that they operate themselves. The staff employed are mainly engaged in maintaining equipment. Everything is centralized to the control room. One main operator can see everything which is taking place in the circuit. He knows the whole story from the boiler room upwards. If anything goes wrong he can see it.

Every part of Goonhilly station, with the exception of the aerial, is duplicated because there is an agreement that this station will be 99.9 per cent effective. If one piece failed, a thousand telephone subscribers would have their conversations chopped. There is a working and a stand-by channel, both of which are automatically 'looked at'; if one channel is not working properly it will be changed over to the stand-by automatically. There are two different sources of power supply so that if one should fail the other can be used. Many of the spares and stand-by equipment are in triplicate.

The buildings are fireproof, so there is no risk of a major fire. In the event of a component becoming faulty it will blow its fuse. Even so, in the unlikely event of anything drastic happening, an alarm bell will ring.

With all these precautions against breakdown, Goonhilly has

the best record of the three ground stations in Europe. It has never had to call on another country for stand-by facilities.

The station was started with the minimum amount of equipment, but this has been multiplied five times and it can still be doubled if and when necessary. At present there are only two aerials, but there is room for five. The second aerial, provided at a cost of two million pounds, was swung into action at the beginning of 1969, after the successful launching of Intelsat III.

Through Intelsat every earth station is joined by teleprinter to every other earth station and to its International Maintenance Control (IMC), with a private line for engineers.

There are two panels which control the transmitter and receiver on the two big aerials, which are a quarter of a mile distant.

A pen chart recorder shows how the station is working and plots those things which would not be seen unless eight men were watching all the time. If the aerial has moved out of track this connection can see it. Every evening a review of the day's activity is held.

As trade increases so does the demand for world-wide telecommunications. Small wonder that earth stations such as Goonhilly command the attention of the world. It has been stated that space research has so far proved more valuable for its contribution to communications than for what it has taught mankind about the universe.

Ideal Home
Exhibition
OLYMPIA, London
March 4th-29th '69

CHAPTER

14

Confravision

One of the problems of modern business is the number of conferences which must, of necessity, take place between top executives, sales and technical staff and others, often entailing long-distance travel and overnight stay at the centre where these are held; an expensive proceeding in time and money.

Confravision has been designed with the object of avoiding this. Basically it is a method of using closed circuit television, but developing and expanding it into a two-way system to suit the requirements of such conferences.

Introduced primarily as a medium of entertainment in the home, television is becoming more and more widely used as an information service in educational studies, medical techniques, security in department stores and the like. Confravision makes use of television for communication, providing a two-way link for the exchange of information and opinions.

As an experiment the Post Office set up two studios in London, one at Telecommunications Headquarters in the City, and the other at Dollis Hill Research Station, the link between the two points costing approximately fifty thousand pounds. These studios have been designed and built under the direction of Post Office engineers at a cost of ten to fifteen thousand pounds each. During the trial period, heads of industry and commerce have been invited to make use of this service and give their opinions as to its practical application to their particular requirements and so assist in a market research programme planned to assess its possibilities. The intention is to provide a network of such studios linked to the principal centres all over the country, giving two-way exchange in sound and vision between one centre and another.

The camera can be set so that one, three or five people can be seen and heard in each soundproof studio as required. Members of the conference sit at a curved console facing the camera, which is flanked by the monitoring television screens on which both parties can be seen. Each person has a private microphone. A flick of a switch is all that is required for the conference to commence. Good picture quality and sound production at normal voice levels are assured. To the left of the studio is a blackboard camera set behind a screen of translucent material on which, by 'throwing' a switch, diagrams, charts and drawings relative to the conference discussion can be made with a felt pen and seen by viewers in both studios at one time. When these drawings are no longer required, the used piece can be torn off the roll, leaving it clear for any further drawings which may be required in the course of the conference.

A sound tape recorder for recording what is said at either end is connected to the system. The document camera contains a 5 : 1 zoom lens which enables print, diagrams, plans or objects to be blown up large so that small details can be seen quite clearly by viewers in both studios. Documents can also be transmitted by facsimile apparatus if a copy is required by the people at the other end, and if more than one copy is required, the transmitted document can be photocopied on a separate machine so that all members of the conference can have a copy within a few minutes of a request being made.

In the studio, but out of view of the television camera, is a console where a secretary can sit and take notes. This console is set in such a position that it is of easy access to the facsimile transmission and photocopying room.

A special switch-box can either be plugged into a socket outlet on the secretary's desk or placed where it can be used by the chairman or another member of the conference. This not only controls the tape recorder but also sound and vision. If private discussion is required in only one of the studios, by means of this switch-box, sound only, or sound and vision, can be cut off as required.

The camera itself is unobtrusive, only the lens being on view through an aperture in the wall. Lighting has been planned at ceiling level so that a good picture is obtained without discomfort to the viewer, while control of air change in air-conditioned studios is so planned that no one need suffer from overheating, and smoking creates no problems.

To ensure that proceedings are conducted in the strictest confidence, 'scrambler' devices can be incorporated into the sound circuit.

The intention is that linked studios shall be set up between two or three of the large cities, for example, between London and Birmingham, with terminals at the Post Office Towers. Studios will be rented on an hourly basis, though it is anticipated that large companies might eventually prefer to set up their own studios after consultation with the Post Office. Cost will, of course, be an important factor in the success of the system, and this obviously must depend on its popularity. A tentative rental charge has been worked out at approximately one hundred and twenty pounds an hour for links of up to one hundred miles, and two hundred pounds an hour for links of two hundred miles, depending on distance between studios.

At first sight this might appear to be an expensive luxury. But if the cost is set against time, travelling and overnight expenses of a number of key executives of a business, it could effect a considerable saving, as well as result in speeding up proceedings.

Indications during this test period are that confravision will quickly become popular, and there is no technical reason why it should not be extended to smaller towns, and links developed with Europe and America.

Once more, as in so many other telecommunications systems, this country has led the way in providing a new public service, for confravision is believed to be the first of its kind in the world.

15

Staff and Training

Although, with the Post Office becoming a National Corporation, staff will no longer be civil servants, there is no reason to suppose that this will materially affect either their work or their status; in fact, with the increasing modernization of the service, more and even better opportunities of promotion could apply.

One of the points which is frequently stressed by the Post Office and its employees is that there are always opportunities of promotion within the service. Many who began their service in the Post Office as postmen, counter clerks, trainees or engineers have come up through different stages of authority as supervisors, inspectors, regional and administrative officials; professional, scientific and research engineers in post and telecommunications. This is made possible by the fact that vacancies are first advertised in Post Office journals so that staff have the opportunity of applying for any position for which they are likely to be suited, before such vacancies are advertised outside.

Another factor which makes promotion possible is the opportunity provided by the Post Office for special courses for higher grade posts. Junior grade engineers, who are without the qualifications required for university education, can apply for a special twelve-week study course at a technical college which covers the academic side of telecommunications and includes mathematics, physics and applied mechanics. Those who complete the course successfully go on to one of the three universities which take technical entrants with a City and Guilds Telecommunications Certificate and 'O' level in English language, but who do not have G.C.E. 'A' level qualifications or the Ordinary National Certificate.

For this degree preparatory course, engineers under thirty years of age are preferred. Those who take the preparatory course are given special leave with full pay for the whole period and are expected to live near the technical college. Other opportunities exist for higher grade staff, such as assistant postal controllers. Such officials may be selected for courses run by business schools in London and Manchester for training as top-class managers.

There are research Fellowships for selected members of staff and post-graduate studies at universities. A student apprenticeship scheme, aimed at producing executive engineers and scientific officers, gives opportunities for high-ranking positions. School leavers and others wishing to become postal clerks or telephonists are trained in special schools set up for the purpose.

Vacancies for telephonists are advertised in the evening papers. In the London area alone there are about seven hundred applicants each week and of these two hundred and fifty will be selected and tested for spelling ability, the pronunciation of British place names and for good hearing and clear speech on the telephone. The applicant being tested for speech and hearing sits at a desk fitted with telephonist's equipment and connected by telephone to a supervisor on the other side of the room, so that the actual conditions of the job are simulated. All successful candidates are required to have a medical examination at the medical unit at the Centre.

Applicants start as ordinary telephonists and have a period of trial before becoming permanent telephonists. They can rise to subbing supervisors, supervisors, divisional supervisors, to chief supervisors.

The National Giro Centre at Bootle has provided many new and interesting jobs for people on Merseyside and other departments of the Post Office. All transaction documents for this new current account banking service are processed by accounting and encoding machines, reading and sorting equipment and by one of the largest computer complexes in Europe. Some 2,500 staff, both men and women, are employed at the Centre and the majority were recruited during the spring and summer of 1968.

New staff receive training either for operating keyboard machines, for clerical jobs, or for work with computers.

This huge Post Office staff, of nearly half a million, includes those from school-leaving age upwards. Such a wide and varied type of work is provided by the Post Office that there is room for men and women and young people with all kinds of experience to progress from one section to another.

In 1906 the Post Office inaugurated an 'awards suggestion scheme'. The number of suggestions made by the staff has increased year by year until nearly five thousand ideas a year are presented. Awards over a recent five-year period total twenty-one thousand two hundred and sixty-eight pounds, with as much as four hundred pounds being paid for one idea which has benefited the work of the Post Office. Only last year a Post office engineer received an award of two hundred and fifty pounds for a device which has improved productivity and resulted in less interruption in telephone services while repair and maintenance work is in progress.

It is difficult to classify a large staff in an organization with such wide ramifications, but in the main it can be said that it is made up of twenty-two thousand postal clerks, fifty-nine thousand telephonists and telephone supervisors, one hundred and twenty thousand engineers of different grades, and one hundred and twenty-five thousand postmen. The remaining staff is made up of professional, administrative and higher clerical officers, typing staff, telegraph, radio and postal supervisors, telegraph and radio operators and miscellaneous and domestic staff. In addition there are the sub-postmasters who are employed on an agency basis.

These headings are only rough guides as to the variety of work done. They can be divided and sub-divided many times and they give opportunities for work all over Britain.

Unions covering different grades of postal and telecommunications employees ensure a fair deal with regard to pay and hours of employment.

All who enter the service of the Post Office, in whatever capacity, are expected to have a sense of social responsibility.

CHAPTER

16

Research and the Future

Computers are playing an increasingly important part in education, commerce, research and industry, and the Post Office is one of the biggest users in the country. In the foreseeable future it is anticipated that telephone lines will be used more for machine language than for voices.

The Post Office has established a series of transmission facilities known as datel services. To do this a range of equipment, working at speeds from fifty signals a second to forty-eight thousand signals a second, has been produced.

Data is computer language, and data transmission is big and successful business today. In data services the aim is to keep errors down to about one in ten million. Data is used in banks, manufacturing and business concerns as well as by specialists in hospitals. The Post Office uses data transmission to deal with the eight hundred thousand postal orders each day, used postal orders being sent to Chesterfield, which office is connected to a computer in London. Serial numbers are fed into the reading machine at Chesterfield and flashed to the computer in the London office, at speeds of three thousand six hundred a minute. This system avoids the laborious task of sorting the postal orders into numerical sequence.

To make this service available to those who require it the Post Office rents out a 'modem', which is a small box for the

115

transmission of data over telephone circuits. This links the data to the ordinary telephone. Two modems are required, one to accept the information from the computer and convert it into electrical signals for transmission over the telephone circuit, while the modem at the receiving end converts the signals back into computer language. Any ordinary telephone fitted with a modem can be switched from speech to data, which can be sent to any telephone fitted with a modem to receive it. Thus, in the case of banks, or sales organizations, any branch can send daily statements or transactions through to their head office by this means even though there is only one computer at that office.

If a branch of a sales organization wishes to advise the management at head office of their sales during the day they can use a telephone with a modem to dial the number required, when the operator at the other end can switch the call to a computer. The caller switches his call to his modem, and data is transmitted over the telephone circuit through the modem which converts the machine language into voice-type signals and back again. The data can be fed in either automatically from magnetic tape, punched tape or punched cards, or manually by someone operating a keyboard. Any information which the caller requires can be transmitted back to him immediately on the same line.

In a hospital theatre an electrocardiogram indicating the condition of a patient's heart, can be connected to a modem. This links the data, or heartbeat, to the ordinary telephone in the theatre. On another phone the doctor can call up a heart specialist who has two telephones, one of which is a modem. The specialist who is being called can pick up the receiver on the phone with the modem, press a button and check the readings as they are reproduced on his own cardiograph. On the other phone he can give his advice to the doctor, based on the patient's condition. This is an exceptional use of data which does not follow the normal process, but it does suggest that data has great possibilities in many fields in the future.

In spite of recent attempts at modernization, both postal and telecommunications systems have still a great deal of equipment to be replaced and much modern machinery to be added before the best and quickest service can be given. This is partly due to shortage of capital. Grants agreed by Parliament for this purpose over the past decade were not ratified and in consequence much out-dated equipment had to be kept in use, although it became phenomenally expensive to run. Telephone switchboards were worn and obsolete, telephones were in short supply with a long waiting list of would-be subscribers in many regions. On the postal side new sorting offices, or adjustments to existing offices to enable modern machinery to be installed, could not be proceeded with.

All this is changing, however. During the next four or five years, two thousand million pounds is to be spent on telecommunications, and two hundred million on the postal services. This is nearly twice as much as that spent on telecommunications in the previous five years, and nearly four times the amount spent in the five years before that. These large sums of money are to be spent on extending the existing telephone network, improving that which is in use, increasing the data and telex systems, and carrying out extensions to schools and other television network auxiliary services. The bulk of the allocation for telecommunications goes in providing new telephone exchanges and supplying the local equipment. Lead sheathed cables do not wear out, but telephone exchanges do.

Mechanization in the postal services, which had just started when war broke out, was halted until 1946, when the new facing machine and segregator were developed. In the 1950's machines were being built for field trials. These were finished in the early 1960's and others were on the stocks for sorting letters to many more destinations and for putting code mark dots on letters.

Among the projects being worked on at the Research Station at Dollis Hill in North London is that of designing a character recognition machine which will automatically recognize the individual character or the complete words in an address on a letter without the intervention of man. It is hoped that, by 1971, this project will be sufficiently advanced for work to commence on such a machine. Already one has been developed in America and tried out in an office; the Japanese also claim that they are developing one.

How is research on such a problem begun? Scientists start with the theory that if man can do it, and it can be understood how he does it, then there must be a possibility that a machine can do it. Man can read typescript, so researchers study how man sets about recognizing what he sees. Though the answer may not be apparent for a long time, at least there are a lot of clues. All who are studying this project work on some variant of the way they think man does it.

While the research is proceeding, the practice of those engaged in it is not to disclose anything to others until sufficient work on the core of the problem has been done to enable it to be patented. Any new machine such as this is first made at the Post Office Research Station at Dollis Hill. After that, relevant industries who will make these machines for the Post Office are shown the specifications and informed of the number required in different towns.

About fourteen hundred large and small contractors supply the new plant and equipment for telecommunications business. These contractors' factories are spread all over the country, the majority of the equipment being produced in development areas.

Besides the anticipated very big increases in telephone users, by 1975 there will be fifty thousand telex connections in service and the same number of datel terminals. Telex traffic is growing by 20 per cent per annum, while this country leads Europe in the provision of datel facilities. Over two thousand much needed new buildings, besides major extensions to existing ones, will be started during the next few years.

Another field in which Britain leads the world is in the development of small to medium electronic exchanges. Electronics provide a faster and more reliable service than mechanical switching. What is more, they can offer a wider range of facilities for new customers. Electronic exchange equipment has increased reliability and does not require so much maintenance. Another of its advantages is that it prevents faulty calls by checking the path before putting a call through and, in the event of a failure, it can find an alternative path. It can even be made to record faults and take a faulty path out of service.

Some of these exchanges are already in use in small towns in counties outside of London, and orders for the manufacture of these are being placed at the rate of one hundred and sixty a year. Thirty-five million pounds will be spent on this equipment over the five-year period.

By 1970 the automatic service will be extended to enable most subscribers to dial practically all their calls in the United Kingdom. STD will be greatly extended by new types of exchange known as 'transit switching' centres. This will facilitate automatic connection from any telephone to any other telephone in the country. The first of these new exchanges was opened in Birmingham this year and some have since been installed in other large towns. The intention is that thirty-seven towns will eventually have these at a cost of seventeen million pounds.

The Post Office is fully aware that improvements in the service to existing customers are very necessary and this, as will be seen from the foregoing, is to have first call on the capital expenditure over the next five years. Additional circuits and new switching equipment will do much to eradicate congestion of calls and so avoid the all too frequent 'engaged' signal being heard during the busiest hours when business and industry most need a speedy and efficient service.

Maintenance techniques are constantly being improved with the object of identifying and forestalling potential faults in existing equipment. Underground cables throughout the trunk and junction network have been protected by air pressurization, which makes it easier to pinpoint cable damage and enables faults to be discovered and remedied before the inner core of the cable is affected. This technique is being extended to the rest of the cable system, thus minimizing fault liability. The beneficial result of this was evident in 1968 during the floods in south-east England, which caused temporary interruption to eight thousand subscribers' lines. Service was restored much more quickly than would have been possible had the cables not been protected in this way.

To provide service of modern standards, even in the remotest dwelling or community, such as the Scottish Highlands and Islands, old submarine cables are being replaced by radio links and, where existing plant is inadequate for present-day needs, additional underground cables and radio links will replace or supplement existing plant. This will result in the extension of dialling facilities to all subscribers in these distant areas.

In many cases, research workers have plenty of ideas on how many things could be developed, but the cost would be pro-hibitive at present. For instance, it would be possible to arrange a system whereby a subscriber could go to the telephone before leaving home in the morning and dial a whole lot of instruc-tions into the instrument, such as where he is going to be, whether he wants to take calls while he is there, whether he is going to allow the children at home to make trunk or local calls, and so on. The system would be so arranged that periodically during the day it would see that calls for the subscriber were re-routed to his golf club or office or private address, and at one o'clock calls could be routed back again. Although such a system has been discussed and is, in fact, technically possible, no nation in the world gives such a service at present because it would be too expensive to be practical. Neither will any nation, with the possible exception of America, place such a scheme high on its priority list.

The Systems Branch deals with projects which are not expected to come to fruition for some years, so far as the sub-scriber is concerned. The staff study the design and per-formance of the instruments, bearing in mind cheapness and reliability in standing up to the problems involved in different offices. They have developed the Loud Speaking Telephone, of which there are about ten thousand in use. They are very satisfactory artistically, but the rental is quite high.

Research workers are endeavouring to make it easier for the customer to use the telephone by means of the push button telephone and the way digits might be placed to make dialling simpler.

Another big branch at the Research Station is dealing with switching. This branch is conducting experiments to improve methods by which signals which have been put into digital or data-like form can be switched to speech. A great deal of the network is capable of carrying twenty-four speech channels on two pairs of wires if in digital form, thus boosting the carrying capacity of existing cables without the costly task of laying new ones.

An ambitious programme is on foot with regard to guided radio signals. These signals are normally sent out into free space, but experiments are being made to find systems by means of which one copper pipe from London to Birmingham would carry all present traffic, including many times more television channels. This copper pipe is hollow, cylindrical and about two inches in diameter. It must not go around corners; but must have only slow bends. The difficulty is to use these slow bends to help it around corners.

Coaxial cable is expensive and bulky, and experiments are being made with optical communications in the form of a new and special form of optical lamp known as a laser. This has a property very valuable to scientists and engineers, making it possible to convey signals by optical means. Post Office research workers are now looking at the possibilities of transmitting along a line of glass fibres, not much thicker than human hairs, with one type of glass for the core surrounded by a different type of glass. They are actually attempting to make glass fibres which can be bent. Glass fibres don't 'talk to each other'— they have nothing to do with their neighbours, which means a whole batch of glass fibres can take the place of and be more useful than coaxial cables. It is hoped to be able to launch an optical signal, varying in intensity, to carry an enormous amount of traffic, but the problem is how to join the fibres together.

Another thing which is engaging the attention of research workers is the form of signals which require to be transmitted to allow for multiple access to a single satellite. A lot of countries can see a satellite over the Atlantic and all these countries want to talk to each other to some extent. For example, America and England want frequent communication, while Venezuela, for example, does not want to talk to these countries so much, but does want to talk to Norway. No one wants to talk to one country through another. With multiple access, any country can obtain access to a satellite according to its needs; every earth station will be on its own. The difficulty which arises is how all earth stations can be fitted in on an economic basis so that they can talk to one another when they want to, but leave the circuits free at certain times of the day so that others may use them. There are plenty of ways of doing this but all are rather expensive. A good technical solution which is biased in favour of neither the big nor the small user must be found. This will be a matter on which the nations of the world will need to get together to find a solution.

Work is progressing on submarine cables to increase still further the number of channels through which speech can be transmitted at the same time, by means of time assignment speech interpolation. This means allowing one subscriber to take another's speech between phases.

A new generation of ultra-long-life transistors is being made by the Post Office. They have to be developed, made and tested to such a degree that the researchers can say they have technical data to prove that not more than one of these transistors will fail in ten years.

These long-life transistors will be used in three North Sea telephone cables planned for the early 1970s, and are guaranteed to last twenty-five years. They will form the 'heart' of the repeaters to be used with the cables, and are made from a chip of silicon smaller than the head of a pin. With their ability to amplify one thousand two hundred and sixty telephone conversations, they will make this submarine telephone cable the largest capacity cable in the world.

Sixteen years ago the Post Office began making its own thermionic valves for undersea cables and encouraging parallel industrial development of these, because devices with a high enough reliability for deep sea use were unobtainable. A single repair in such cases could cost over two hundred and fifty thousand pounds in lost revenue. Of the three thousand long life valves made by the Post Office over the years, and put into service in deep water, there has been only one failure in one hundred and forty-five million valve hours of service. Transistors offer advantages of even greater reliability and circuit capacity, and the Post Office is now among the world leaders in this field.

These new transistors have been developed at Dollis Hill and here, where they are made, extraordinary steps are taken to make sure they come up to the guaranteed standard. Wastage is high; for every five hundred transistors required, up to ten thousand have to be made. A failure in one device could mean a whole batch has to be rejected. The transistors for the new North Sea cables are to be given a six months' laboratory 'systems trial' which is equivalent to about four years' operation.

Stringent precautions are taken in the temperature- and humidity-controlled laboratory where the transistors are made. Engineers have to change into special clothing. Filtered air is blown across their benches, for one speck of dust could ruin a transistor. If anyone wants to sneeze he has to go to a special 'sneeze hatch' in the laboratory's air exhaust system!

For years scientists and research technicians have been engaged in seeking means of reducing the amount of equipment required in telecommunications systems. First there were valves, then transistors, which are so widely used today. Now there are micro circuits, which are many times smaller than transistors. The design, reliability and performance of these are studied at Dollis Hill.

Another department makes a study of human factors: customers' reaction to the delay in speech by satellite, which can be overcome, to some extent, by communicating one way by satellite and one way by cable. This department is also responsible for the quality of television pictures put out; providing as good a quality picture as is consistent with the low cost which the B.B.C. and independent companies can afford to pay. An assessment on colour television is also being made by this department.

The viewphone, or person-to-person television, is something else on which tests are being made. The standards in this country are different from those in America and agreement will have to be reached on these so that world standards can be set up. It is expected that this television phone will be perfected within the next ten years. In fact, the telephone line will become the most important link between the home and the outside world. It will have an attachment available for all kinds of communications, such as bank statements and invoices. It will even provide remote control of machinery.

The Postmaster General has felt sufficiently confident of the development of communications to forecast an explosion of these during the next ten years, with computers talking to computers at a rapid pace over a communication network.

The Post Office Research Station, which has been situated at Dollis Hill in North London for many years, is to be replaced by a multi-million-pound station at Martlesham Heath, near Ipswich. This ninety-eight-acre site is being planned for almost every kind of experimental work and there will be space outside for field trials. There will be an administrative block as well as a seven-storey laboratory block and research services centre. Work has started on this project, which will have a staff of two thousand.

Of all the public services which benefit the average citizen, that involving the means of communicating with others is one of the most vital. When the Union of Post Office Workers, in January 1969, withdrew the labour of its Overseas Telegraph Operator members, this not only affected overseas telecommunications but caused delay in certain areas of the postal service. Fortunately the stoppage was both limited and short lived, but the dislocation of business and industry, both here and overseas, which would result from the complete interruption of Posts and Telecommunications, even for a limited period, is something which it is to be hoped would never happen.

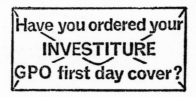

Have you ordered your INVESTITURE GPO first day cover?

Index

Compensation, claims for, 7
Computer language, 115, 116, 124
Computers, 9, 28, 75, 76, 80, 93, 101, 104, 113, 115, 116
Confravision, 3, 107–10
Consultancy service, 38
Corbould, Henry, 15
Cordless switchboards, 70
Crown offices, 4, 5, 12
Customs, 32

Damaged mail, 32
Data, 9, 115–17, 121
Data transmission, 115, 116
Datel services, 115, 118
Dead Letter Office. *See* Returned Letter Branch
Death duty, stamps and documents, 11
Decca, 85
Decimalization, 17
Delays, 2, 5
Delivery of letters, 1, 12, 18, 37, 38
Demand Trunk Dialling, 73
Dial-a-disc, 78
Dialling, 73–5, 78, 80, 91, 93, 98, 120
Design of postage stamps, 14, 15, 18
Detector vans, 11
Directories, telephone, 65, 76, 77, 80
Directory Enquiries, 74, 76, 77
Disabled subscribers, 66
Dockwra, William, 24
Dog licences, 11

Drivers, van, 28
Driving licences, 11
Drugs sent through post, 32
Dynamometers, 82, 85, 87, 88

Early Bird, 102, 103
Earth stations, 3, 101, 103, 105, 106, 122
Echo, 1, 2, 102
Edison, Thomas, 56
Electrocardiogram, 116
Electronic exchanges, 70, 80, 118, 119
Electronic letter sorter, 49
Engraving of postage stamps, 15
Envelopes, accounts, 75
business reply, 18
empty, 14
Post Office Preferred, 53
registered, 7
stamped, 16
Error correction equipment, 61
Exchanges, telephone, 61, 65, 66, 69, 70, 72, 73, 80, 90, 96, 98, 117–19
Exhibition: Post Office, 64
Telecommunications, 65, 67
Expenditure, postal, 1, 48, 117
Express letters, 1
messengers, 35

Facing of letters, 31
Facing machines, Facer, 33, 51, 117